Enterprise
Risk Management

Third Edition

Steven M. Bragg

AccountingTools®

For more information about AccountingTools® products, visit our Web site at www.accountingtools.com.

ISBN-13: 978-1-64221-068-2

Printed in the United States of America

Table of Contents

i

Preface

The typical business is subject to a broad array of risks, including product failures, foreign currency exchange rates, floods, hail storms, and losing key employees. Some of these risks can be eliminated by purchasing insurance, but many cannot. Instead, a business must find ways to offset or avoid risks. It can also choose to selectively accept certain risks in exchange for targeted business opportunities, such as entering into a new and unexplored market. *Enterprise Risk Management* shows how to identify and sort through these risks and deal with each one.

The book is divided into two sections. In Chapters 1 through 10, we provide an overview of risk management and then focus on the risks found in each functional area of an organization, including treasury, sales and marketing, the supply chain, and human resources. The intent is to identify risks and note ways to mitigate them. In Chapters 11 through 13, we deal with more specialized topics, which are insurance, the incorporation of risk into various financial analyses, and the measurement and reporting of risk.

You can find the answers to many questions about enterprise risk management in the following chapters, including:

- How is risk incorporated into the strategy of a business?
- How can the risk of not obtaining funding be reduced in a tight credit market?
- What are the alternative methods for reducing interest rate risk?
- What risks are associated with the supply chain?
- How can the risk of not being able to recruit qualified job candidates be reduced?
- What types of risks are associated with the information technology area?
- What types of business entities present the least risk of loss for the investor?
- Which terms and conditions are commonly inserted into insurance contracts?
- How can risk considerations be included in price setting?
- What are the core reports needed for management to monitor key risks?

Enterprise Risk Management is designed primarily for professionals, who can use it as a reference tool for setting up a risk management system and monitoring the status of risks throughout an organization.

Centennial, Colorado
June 2021

About the Author

Steven Bragg, CPA, has been the chief financial officer or controller of four companies, as well as a consulting manager at Ernst & Young. He received a master's degree in finance from Bentley College, an MBA from Babson College, and a Bachelor's degree in Economics from the University of Maine. He has been a two-time president of the Colorado Mountain Club, and is an avid alpine skier, mountain biker, and certified master diver. Mr. Bragg resides in Centennial, Colorado. He has written more than 250 books and courses, including *New Controller Guidebook*, *GAAP Guidebook*, and *Payroll Management*.

Steven maintains the accountingtools.com web site, which contains continuing professional education courses, the Accounting Best Practices podcast, and thousands of articles on accounting subjects.

Chapter 1
Risk Management Overview

Introduction

Risk equates to uncertainty regarding a future outcome. A business is filled with uncertainty, for there are few situations in which the outcome can be predicted with complete reliability. For example, a business has several thousand outstanding accounts receivable – exactly how many of them will become bad debts? Similarly, a business requires a key commodity as a raw material in the construction of a product – can it predict exactly what the price of this commodity will be in one year? Or, it will cost $250 million to develop a new drug and have it approved – but how certain is the approval? In these cases, it is impossible to predict the exact outcome.

Uncertainty is pervasive, and yet managers routinely ignore the concept of variable outcomes. Instead, they use budgets to derive a single view of the future, and are then perturbed when they cannot force their organizations to deliver results that precisely match the outcome predicted in the budget. This is because there may be thousands of uncertain events that all impact the financial results of a business. Despite management's best efforts, it is nearly impossible to deliver actual results that match the original budgeted prediction.

A better way to see the impact of risk is to view an organization as a portfolio of risks, each of which is derived from any number of management decisions made in the past. Some decisions, such as expanding an existing product line, are more likely to result in modest profits or losses. Other decisions, such as the funding of a portable fusion reactor product, could be spectacularly successful or drive a firm into bankruptcy. Some may produce offsetting gains and losses, resulting in modest net changes. One should be cognizant of the more crucial of these risks, sometimes to take advantage of them and at other times to reduce them.

In this chapter, we describe the concept of risk management, how to incorporate it into an organization's overall strategy, who is responsible for it, the risk management process, and contingency planning.

Benefits of Risk Management

There are a number of reasons why an organization should manage its risks. The central issues are the ability to smooth out earnings or to enhance earnings.

Risk management can be used to mitigate the occurrence of unusual expenses, so that the actual expenses incurred are much closer to budgeted expectations. This is particularly important for a publicly held company, which can then give the investment community reliable guidance about its future results. When a business consistently reports earnings that do not vary much from predictions, investors will probably keep the stock price within a relatively narrow range, and there will be no reason for any investors to engage in short selling. Another benefit is that reliable earnings attract lenders, so that a business is more likely to be offered reasonable interest rates and longer-term lending arrangements. Lower interest rates reduce the cost of a firm's capital, so that it can invest in more projects that have lower projected returns. Having longer-term debt arrangements means that a business can more easily weather market crises, since it does not have to constantly roll over its debt into new loans.

One can enhance earnings by actively identifying opportunities that are risky, but which also generate high returns. For example, an organization might choose to start doing business in a country where profits could be substantial, but where there is also a risk of a currency devaluation. Taking this approach can result in higher profits, but those profits are also likely to be more variable – very high in some periods, but with notable losses in others. This use of risk management works well when the management team is willing to aggressively pursue profits.

The most likely scenario in a well-managed business is that management takes advantage of both types of risk management. They are well aware of the risks to which the business is subjected, and take steps to mitigate risks in certain areas while accepting the risk associated with selected business opportunities.

The amount of risk taken on by a business depends on the comfort level of the management team. Some may prefer a highly stable environment from which the probability of risk has largely been reduced, while others are more comfortable taking large chances throughout the organization in order to pursue the possibility of maximizing profits.

The Interrelationship between Risk and Strategy

The two preceding benefits of risk management can be incorporated into an entity's strategic planning. When the management team considers the strategic direction of a business, a major part of the analysis should center on the risks that are linked to each possible strategic alternative, and how to handle those risks. Since there may be a number of strategic alternatives with many risks attached to each one, the planners will need to focus on just the most critical risks associated with each strategy, and develop the following information:

- The likelihood of occurrence
- The cost per occurrence
- Mitigation alternatives

Ideally, each proposed strategy should outline key risks, how risks are to be mitigated or off-loaded, *or* the cost of retaining the risks. The senior management team can then review this risk summary as part of its analysis of strategic alternatives.

Tip: When evaluating the risks associated with strategic alternatives, consider any circumstances that could amplify the likelihood or cost of risks. If the amplified risk turns out to have a massive loss potential, this could influence the decision to avoid a strategic direction.

Risk Retention Strategy

Not all risks can be successfully mitigated. Some types of risk can be expensive to guard against, perhaps with relatively expensive hedging contracts. Consequently, there should be some level of risk that it is more economical over the long-term for a business to retain.

The amount of risk that a business is willing to retain is strongly influenced by its financial position. For example, a company with significant market share, profitability, and cash reserves can easily withstand the financial losses associated with risk. Conversely, a company that is highly leveraged and which uses much of its cash to pay off loan principal can afford to retain very little risk.

This ability to retain risk can have a profound impact on the overall strategy of a business. In essence, a financially stable entity is in a much better position to dabble in new lines of business that offer major upside potential, but which also run the risk of significant losses.

EXAMPLE

The management team of the thermometer manufacturer Kelvin Corporation has just completed a leveraged buyout of the founder, which involves taking on $10 million of high-cost debt that must be paid off within the next five years. For this period, the sole focus of the management team is on paying off the debt. The company cannot afford to risk any funds on new product development.

At the same time, Celsius Corporation has just raised money through a major new stock offering, and is risking $5 million on the development of a new lineup of remote temperature sensors that use the theory of quantum entanglement to track temperature readings from thousands of miles away. There is a significant risk that the development project will fail, but the upside potential is complete patent protection in a large new market.

Given the financial circumstances of the two companies, Kelvin cannot afford to take on any risk, while the management of Celsius has so much money that it can take on highly risky projects.

Risk Analysis as an Opportunity

The analysis of potential risk to which a business is subjected should not be a casual affair, but rather a studied one. This means keeping a running list of problems that other companies have encountered within the industry and in adjacent industries, and reviewing the list at regular intervals to see if events have made any risks more or less likely.

The identification of risks may present opportunities; a company could launch initiatives in new areas that competitors might consider excessively risky. This is particularly likely when a higher level of risk is accompanied by a greater chance of reward.

EXAMPLE

There is a general dearth of storefronts near a certain section of coastline, since it has been hit by three hurricanes in the past ten years. A real estate company is fully aware of the hurricane risk, and develops a new building design that mitigates the risk of storm damage by elevating the first floor of the building, leaving room for storm waters to flow under the building. The company successfully builds and operates these structures, which survive several additional hurricanes with minimal damage. In this case, the company is fully aware of the risks, and chooses to proceed in a manner that mitigates those risks.

EXAMPLE

A CPA firm has just been devastated by a major tornado that wiped out a large part of the city in which it is located. It could take the prudent path of following the other CPA firms out of town, to relocate to a safer city. Instead, the partners decide to construct a robust safe room for the employees that will also contain client files, and markets this upgrade as a document storage facility for clients. The result is a major boost in business, especially since most of the other CPA firms have fled the city.

A reverse way of looking at risk-related opportunities is to evaluate when to exit an excessively staid business. A low-risk environment tends to also generate low returns, so it can make sense to see if any product lines or customers that have a combination of low risk and low reward should be eliminated.

EXAMPLE

Gulf Coast Insurance is evaluating its hurricane insurance to see if there are any opportunities to improve its overall rate of return. An examination by geographic region discovers that the Tallahassee area has not borne the brunt of a hurricane for some time, which has resulted in a gradual decline in the insurance rates that can be competitively set in this area. Management concludes that the margins are too low in this region, so it elects not to renew policies in this area, and instead focuses its sales force on other areas where the claim risk is higher, but where prices are also higher.

Special Risk Situations

A business is at its most vulnerable when it is just beginning, since there is likely to be very little capital invested. In this state, even a minor perturbation in the business model could cause the entity to collapse. The situation is worsened by the management team's lack of knowledge of their business environment. They are probably figuring out how their chosen niche works as they develop the business, and so are surrounded by uncertainty.

In this situation, it is absolutely necessary to be aware of the risks to which the business is subjected, and mitigate them to the greatest extent possible. Given the minimal amount of capital available that can be used to absorb losses, the management team cannot afford to leave any significant risk unaddressed.

An organization may find great success if it concentrates its efforts into a small niche area. By doing so, it can build great expertise and tightly focused products that competitors cannot match. However, this success comes at a price, for it may also mean that there are only a small number of potential customers. If so, the firm might find that it is granting large amounts of credit to a small number of customers. If one of these customers cannot pay on time (or at all), the business could be in serious financial trouble.

This situation illustrates an inherent risk of concentrating too tightly on a market niche. To reduce the risk, it may be necessary to expand an organization's business somewhat to encompass an adjacent niche that will increase the number of customers.

Risk Management for the Enterprise

We have just established that the management team should be highly cognizant of the risks to which their organization is subjected. How is this risk to be managed? At the lowest level of effectiveness, those managers who accept the concept of risk will monitor and act on it within their departments. However, this is not especially effective, since some departments are not addressing risk at all, and there is no consistency in the measurements and actions taken even in those situations where department managers are actively pursuing risk management. Worse yet, there is no recognition of risks that occur across multiple departments. In these cases, a risk may appear to be minimal when considered separately in several departments, and yet is a serious concern when viewed in aggregate. These issues lead us to the conclusion that the only way to effectively deal with risk is in a coordinated manner, across the entire enterprise. This concept is called enterprise risk management, or ERM.

An ERM system provides a consistent methodology for locating, measuring, and reporting on risks throughout an organization. It is also used to consider the impact of macroeconomic effects on an entire business, such as changes in interest rates, commodity prices, and inflation rates on the business as a whole. Further, the system provides for a central coordinating authority in the person of a chief risk officer (CRO). The CRO position is described in the next section.

ERM considers the effects of risk across an entire enterprise. When risk is mitigated at the local level, it is entirely possible that derivatives and insurance will be used in excessive amounts, which would be reduced if local managers were aware of countervailing transactions elsewhere in the business. For example, one business unit might be liable for a payment of $100,000 Canadian dollars in three months, and so plans to hedge the transaction. However, a different unit might expect to receive an $80,000 payment in Canadian dollars at the same time (which it plans to hedge), so the net amount at risk is only $20,000 Canadian dollars. From the perspective of the local business units, the company will be paying for hedges of $180,000 Canadian dollars, whereas from an ERM perspective, it would be apparent that the amount to be hedged should be only $20,000 Canadian dollars. Thus, ERM is useful for identifying residual risk, which can be much less expensive to deal with.

The Chief Risk Officer

The chief risk officer (CRO) of a business is considered a mid-level to senior-level manager. This individual may work alone in a smaller organization, or have a staff in a larger, multi-location enterprise. The CRO oversees the following activities:

- Create an integrated risk framework for the entire organization
- Assess risk throughout the organization
- Quantify risk limits
- Develop plans to mitigate risks
- Advise on directing capital to projects based on risk
- Assist functional managers in obtaining risk mitigation funding
- Monitor the progress of risk mitigation activities
- Create and disseminate risk measurements and reports
- Communicate to key stakeholders regarding the risk profile of the business

The CRO may be assigned a number of additional tasks besides the main ones already noted. They include:

- *Oversee insurance*. Decide upon the types and specifics of the various insurance policies that the organization should buy. This includes being the contact person for the insurance providers.
- *Recommend insurance alternatives*. Recommend any alternative insurance features that are not currently being used, or suggest using insurance products that are entirely new to the company.
- *Manage claims*. Supervise the filing of insurance claims, monitor their progress with insurers, and verify that payments have been received.
- *Conduct due diligence*. Investigate the risks inherent in a target company that may be acquired, as well as the state of its risk management practices.

None of the preceding activities place direct responsibility for risk mitigation on the CRO. Instead, the CRO is considered to be an advisory position that brings risk issues to the attention of the rest of the organization.

The interaction of the CRO with local managers can be a difficult one, since the CRO is a staff position that is not responsible for the performance of the individual departments. There are several ways to deal with this situation. One is to act as an in-house resource, where the CRO and any supporting staff work with the departments to create effective control systems. This method tends to foster communication and result in risk management activities that take into account the specific needs of each business unit. However, it may require that the CRO's staff be permanently positioned within the business units, which can detract from the risk management group's independence and objectivity.

Another approach to business unit interaction is to set policies for what is allowed and not allowed, and then act as a policeman to enforce these rules; this can result in adversarial relations, especially when the CRO is seen as restricting the profit-making activities of a business unit. Also, when individuals are penalized by the CRO, there is a strong tendency to hide one's actions, so that news of risky behavior may never find its way to the CRO.

Since the CRO position is essentially an advisory one, this individual needs strong support from the chief executive officer (CEO), or is at risk of being ignored by the other managers. Consequently, the CEO needs to publicly voice his or her support of risk management, while also integrating an emphasis on risk management into the company's reporting structure and performance management system. The CEO's efforts will have succeeded when risk issues are naturally included in the daily discussion of operations amongst the management team.

A continuing question is to whom the CRO should report. A common approach is for this position to report to the general counsel. This places an emphasis on the reactive function of the general counsel, where the focus is on reducing liabilities throughout a business. An alternative is to have the CRO report to the chief strategy officer or the chief operating officer. This approach shifts the orientation of the CRO in the direction of how to deal with the future state of the business, which is a more proactive view of how risk is to be incorporated into an entity.

A key concern when determining a reporting relationship for the CRO is that the senior management team may itself be causing a business to take on an unacceptable amount of risk. For example, if the CEO is determined to triple sales, this may require the business to sell to much riskier customers. Given this possibility, the CRO could be rendered ineffective by reporting to anyone in the management group. Under this scenario, it could make sense to have the CRO report either directly to the board of directors or a committee of the board. However, doing so means that the board must take on the extra responsibilities of hiring and firing the CRO, and of setting this person's compensation.

Risk Management Committee

The CRO chairs a risk management committee, which must make final determinations regarding whether risks should be mitigated or accepted. If risks are to be mitigated, the committee must also decide how this is to be done (such as buying insurance). Given the ramifications of these decisions, the members of the committee should be drawn from the senior management team. These decisions cannot be forced down further into the organization, given the potential size of the financial and operational ramifications.

If the risk management committee is sufficiently broad-based, it can also be used as a general support mechanism for risk management throughout a business. For example, if the heads of all major departments are members of the committee, it is much easier for this group to enforce a general sense of risk awareness among their subordinates.

Given the preceding point about the need for broad participation in the committee, we suggest that the following individuals be members:

- *Chief operating officer.* This person is at least responsible for production and materials management, which covers supply chain risks and a number of internal risk issues.
- *Chief financial officer.* This person is responsible for both treasury and accounting, where many financial risks arise, and so is among the most critical members.
- *Vice president of sales.* This person is responsible for relations with customers, and so must be aware of risk issues arising from that direction.
- *Vice president of strategic planning.* The development of strategic plans requires a detailed knowledge of the risks that arise from each possible strategic direction to be taken or avoided.
- *Vice president of human resources.* Many types of risks are associated with the hiring, treatment, and deployment of personnel, for which this person is either directly responsible or has an advisory role.
- *Internal audit manager.* This person is deeply involved in the corporate system of controls and ongoing testing of it, and so has a daily involvement with systems-related risks.

Finally, the chief executive officer should certainly be a member of the committee, since the risk outcomes of a business can have a profound impact on its financial results and ability to stay in business.

Responsibility for Risk

We have already pointed out that the CRO is really present to place an emphasis on risk within a business, but is not actually responsible for it – indeed, the position does not have sufficient authority to have ultimate responsibility. The trouble is that risk is so pervasive within an organization that no one individual can solely generate an effective and company-wide approach to risk mitigation. Instead, a number of people must be involved. These individuals include:

1. *Functional managers.* Ultimately, those in the best position to enact risk mitigation tactics are those managers directly responsible for functional areas, such as the managers of the treasury, production, and sales departments. These individuals already have direct control over their areas of responsibility, and so can readily add risk management to their portfolios.
2. *Advisors.* The functional managers may not have enough expertise to deal with risk issues by themselves, and so may need to call in specialists to advise them on the best actions to take. For example, a consultant may be hired to advise on the legal aspects of environmental remediation liabilities, or an insurance advisor is called in to discuss the standard exclusions from flood insurance.

3. *Chief risk officer.* The CRO coordinates the general risk management effort, which may include bringing in advisors for the functional managers. However, the CRO is removed somewhat from actually taking action regarding risk, and so is third in this priority listing.

4. *Chief executive officer.* The CEO is ultimately responsible for all actions taken, and so has a strong incentive to authorize significant actions to deal with risk. Nonetheless, this person is well away from the actual management of risk, and so is listed fourth in priority for risk management.

5. *Board of directors.* This group may have a risk committee, and may directly supervise the CRO. In addition, the board sets the tone throughout the organization for how risk is to be dealt with. For the board to be effective in this area, it should be well-trained in risk management concepts, meet frequently enough to stay abreast of risk issues, and routinely question management about how it is dealing with risk. It is also helpful if the board members come from outside the organization and have no financial ties to it, since they can then be more objective in examining how the firm is managed.

The individuals noted in the preceding list are much more likely to take action regarding a risk situation if they hear about the problem. Ensuring that the responsible parties are notified of issues is a real concern, since information about problems tends to remain in the lower levels of many organizations. This issue can be counteracted by constantly communicating the need to push this information up to senior management. Also, it helps to have a flat corporate hierarchy, where there are fewer levels of management between front-line workers and senior management.

Risk Management by the Individual Employee

Risk issues pervade every organization, so it makes little sense to assume that the small number of people listed in the last section will be the only ones actively involved in risk management. Instead, every employee in the organization should be cognizant of risk issues. This does not mean that a massive training program be implemented that forces everyone to learn detailed mathematical analysis models. However, it *does* mean that employees should learn to question transactions based on just a few general risk guidelines. By doing so, they may be able to flag issues that can then be analyzed in greater detail by someone with more experience and training. Here are several guidelines that employees can use:

- How probable is an event? Some events are quite frequent, to the point where allowances for them are included in the annual budget, such as bad debts and inventory theft losses. Other items are considered quite rare, but would be so catastrophic that risk planning for them must be conducted – such as having a backup supplier in case a major supplier's facility is destroyed.

- What is the exposure period? If the period of time during which an event might occur is quite short, the risk level is reduced – with the reverse being the case for a longer period of time. For example, a collector is faced with the choice of being paid only half the amount due by a financially troubled customer right now, or in monthly installments for the full amount over the next three years. The correct choice may be to take the half payment now, since the customer could fail at any time during the next three years.

- What is the maximum amount that could be lost? Large numbers of possible transactions involve quite small amounts, and so present minimal amounts of risk. For example, the theft of a petty cash box only involves a few hundred dollars. However, a request by a customer to expand the current credit line by $100,000 increases the potential loss by $100,000, and so is worthy of much more attention.
- How variable are the potential outcomes? If there have historically been minor fluctuations in the outcome of an event, chances are that the variability of the outcome will continue to be small, which represents a small amount of risk. For example, the occasional currency crisis has caused various exchange rate pairings to fluctuate substantially. Conversely, having a large number of wealthy customers may have resulted in infinitesimal bad debt losses, so that the outcome of extending credit to these customers is considered to be barely variable at all.

Employees could address all of the preceding issues on a regular basis and even with some enthusiasm, but only if they see ongoing support from the management team. For example, if an employee in the treasury department speculates in derivative instruments in order to achieve exceptional returns, how will she be dealt with? If management chooses to ignore the risks being taken because of the high returns, other employees will see that the new focus on risk management is just talk, and will probably not bother themselves with it any further.

Types of Risks

Any company is subject to a large number of risks. To better understand them, it is useful to classify them into different categories. By doing so, one can adopt category-specific tactics to mitigate or transfer risk. Common risk categories are:

Business risk – The organization does not generate sufficient financial results to satisfy its owners. For example:

- A business reports unusually low earnings per share, resulting in the sale of its shares by many investors, which lowers the share price substantially.
- A retailer reports a decline in same-store sales, after which investors vote for a change in the board of directors, which in turn fires the entire management team.

Compliance risk – The organization violates the law, and incurs penalties as a result. For example:

- An airline suffers from several plane crashes. A government probe finds that the airline was skimping on its maintenance procedures, and forcibly shuts down the business.
- An oil drilling company suffers a major underwater drilling failure, resulting in a million-barrel oil spill into the ocean. The affected government immediately sues the company for several billion dollars.

Credit risk – The organization's customers, suppliers, or counterparties to other transactions do not meet their obligations to the business. For example:

- A major customer goes bankrupt, leaving the seller with a massive bad debt that likely cannot be recovered.
- A supplier takes a large advance payment for a custom order and then goes bankrupt, leaving the buyer with little prospect for a recovery.
- A supplier is only able to ship part of an order to the buyer, because it does not have sufficient cash to buy the raw materials needed to complete the order, resulting in disruptions in the buyer's operations.

Liquidity risk – The organization does not have sufficient cash to meet its obligations. For example:

- A company grows so fast that its working capital requirements soak up all available cash. As a result, the business cannot pay its employees, so a competitor scoops up the firm during bankruptcy proceedings.
- The credit market unexpectedly tightens, so that a company cannot renew its line of credit or find an alternative lender.
- A company's credit rating is unexpectedly downgraded, making it much more difficult to sell bonds to investors.

Market risk – The market prices of goods and services, loans and investments, and other financial instruments that an organization depends on move in an unfavorable direction. For example:

- A company takes on a large amount of short-term debt in order to fund a production line expansion. Interest rates then increase, and the company finds that its new venture does not return enough cash to pay the higher interest rate.
- A company buys expensive equipment from a foreign supplier. By the time the invoice is due for payment, the relevant foreign exchange rate has moved sharply in an unfavorable direction, resulting in a much larger amount for the company to pay.

- A business buys petroleum products in bulk and converts them into plastic goods. Its input prices can vary substantially, while it is constrained from passing price increases through to its customers.

Operating risk – The organization suffers losses from failures by its employees, processes, or systems. Acts of nature fall into this category. For example:

- A treasury employee manages to transfer several million dollars of company money to his private account in Grand Cayman.
- Flooding in Thailand destroys a factory that a business was depending on for the electronic components used in its products.
- A bank's computer system crashes, wiping out the records of its depositors and borrowers.

The most dangerous type of risk is *strategic risk*, which interferes with a company's business model. A strategic risk undermines the value proposition which attracts customers and generates profits. For example, if a company's business model is to be the low-cost provider of a product and a competitor from a low-wage country suddenly enters the market, the company will find that its value proposition has been destroyed. Examples of strategic risk scenarios are:

- A new product fails catastrophically
- A major acquisition fails
- A customer gains massive market share and then has an inordinate ability to set prices
- A supplier gains monopoly control over supplies and raises raw material prices
- A key product goes off patent
- There is a sudden shift in technology that makes the company's products obsolete
- The contamination of company products with a hazardous substance leads to brand erosion
- The government changes its tax policy, which eliminates a key pricing advantage built into a firm's business model
- A trade agreement reduces barriers to entry, resulting in a flood of new competitors into the market
- Company assets are nationalized
- Terrorist attacks reduce sales or destroy property

The types of risks to which a business is subjected will vary considerably by company, since risk is based on such factors as geography, industry, product type, and employee relations. Thus, the risk mix is unique to every business. For example, a mining company is subject to the risk of a local shutdown by people who object to local pollution issues, while a business in the apparel industry may face a customer revolt over the working conditions of employees at its foreign clothing factories.

Now that we have a general knowledge of the types of risks to which a business is subjected, we will review the process needed to manage those risks.

The Risk Management Process Flow

There should be a consistent process for identifying, quantifying, and dealing with risk. A more scattershot approach is likely to result in significant risks never being addressed. The general flow to follow is:

1. *Identify risks.* This can involve employee surveys or questionnaires, and/or the use of consultants who have a deep knowledge of the industry. If the management team has many years of experience in the industry, it might limit itself to using internal meetings to derive risks, without polling employees outside of this group. It is useful to view an organization from many perspectives to extract all possible risks. For example:

    *   *Internal capacity.* Are the various functional areas of the company able to handle increased sales or other types of transactions? For example, what would happen to the accounting department's ability to operate if management were to engage in a minimum of three acquisitions per year?
    *   *Inherent internal risks.* Are there risks that "come with the territory" in certain departments; these risks cannot be sidestepped or mitigated. For example, there is a high risk of losing IT personnel, due to shortages in the market for their skills.
    *   *Impact of supply chain.* What would be the impact on the business if a major supplier or the supplier of a strategic part were unable to make deliveries? For example, a supplier might be purchased by a competitor, which intends to reserve all of the supplier's output for itself.
    *   *Impact of customers.* Is the business able to support additional customers? For example, how would the organization deal with the demands of a large retail chain? There may not be sufficient customer service personnel, and returns may increase by several orders of magnitude.
    *   *Future trends.* Are there discernible trends that can alter risks? For example, will the increased amount of social media usage increase the number of poor on-line reviews for a business?
    *   *Historical risks.* Comb through the industry records to see if certain risks have appeared, even if only a few times or just once. The circumstances may change enough for these issues to appear again, though perhaps in a modified form.
    *   *Competitor risks.* Are competitors noting any unusual risks in their financial reports or investor communications? If so, these risks may soon trouble a company's own operations.

These risks can be summarized into a risk profile, which is described later in the Risk Profile sub-section.

2. *Rank risks.* There may be hundreds of possible risks that could impact an organization, so they must be prioritized to focus attention on the key items. This is typically based on their frequency and severity, which can be plotted on a grid that uses frequency and severity as the axes. Severity can be measured by conducting a what-if analysis that reveals the full impact of a risk event on a business. The outcome should show the extent of losses and any reduction of cash reserves.

3. *Mitigate risks.* There are a variety of internal actions that can be taken to mitigate risk, such as moving a factory away from a flood plain or selling off a subsidiary that might otherwise be nationalized. Or, if there is a risk of product failure in the marketplace, consider developing two products at the same time. As another example, the risk of expropriation can be dealt with by halting the investment in the at-risk country or even selling off facilities in that country.

4. *Accept risks.* The likely payout from a risk may be so small that the company can easily bear the risk of loss. Alternatively, the offsetting amount of profit may be so high that the company is willing to accept a substantial amount of risk. For example, there could be a potential for massive profits from a new technology, though the development process could fail.

5. *Transfer risk.* If management cannot mitigate a risk and is unwilling to accept it, the remaining option is to transfer it to another party, usually an insurer. See the Insurance chapter for more information.

6. *Report on the status of risks.* The management team must know if risks are changing, especially in a more frequent or more severe direction. Accordingly, there should be a reporting system in place that focuses attention on key risk "movers," without bogging down the reporting with other risks whose status is unchanged. In addition, a decision must be made about the frequency of reporting. Excessively frequent reporting may be ignored, while reports issued at long intervals may allow new risks to fester without proper management attention.

7. *Repeat.* Repeat the process at regular intervals and especially when there are major changes in a business that might strip away existing risks or introduce new ones, such as entry into a new market or the launch of a new product line. The iterative nature of the risk management process flow cannot be overemphasized, since an organization can learn from its actions in previous iterations to arrive at better risk management solutions in the future.

Tip: Be sure to disseminate risk reports not only upward to senior management, but also across the organization to everyone who is directly responsible for a specific risk. This may call for the production of many individualized versions of the report that are tailored to the recipients.

Risk Rankings

The ranking of risks can be difficult, for they cannot always be quantified. For example, the risk of a product recall can probably be quantified in terms of a range of product repair costs, but cannot be quantified in terms of the damage to the brand. The first figure could be reliably stated as falling somewhere between $800,000 and $1,000,000, but the cost of brand damage could extend for years and involve many lost customers who will no longer automatically turn to the company for replacement products. Consequently, an analysis of the frequency and severity of risks will require a significant amount of judgment, rather than hard numerical analysis. This hardly means that a ranking system should be ignored – judgment can be based on many years of experience, and may result in risk rankings that prove to be fairly accurate.

Given the difficulty of quantification, it can be difficult to assemble an exact ranking of which specific risks are more critical than others. Instead, it can make more sense to use a simple scale to measure a risk's frequency and severity, and concentrate attention on the cluster of risks that score the highest. We illustrate this concept in the following chart, which uses a zero-to-five scale to rate each risk.

Note in the sample table that there is a clear differentiation between three key risks (supplier damage, delivery disruptions, and bottleneck issues) and the remaining risk topics, which would certainly direct management's attention toward these items. At a lesser degree of risk, the chart shows a high frequency for commodity price swings, as well as high severity levels for hurricanes at one location and the risk of a pollution-related shutdown. The remaining risks are a combination of low severity and low frequency, and so would likely receive less management attention.

Sample Risk Rankings Chart

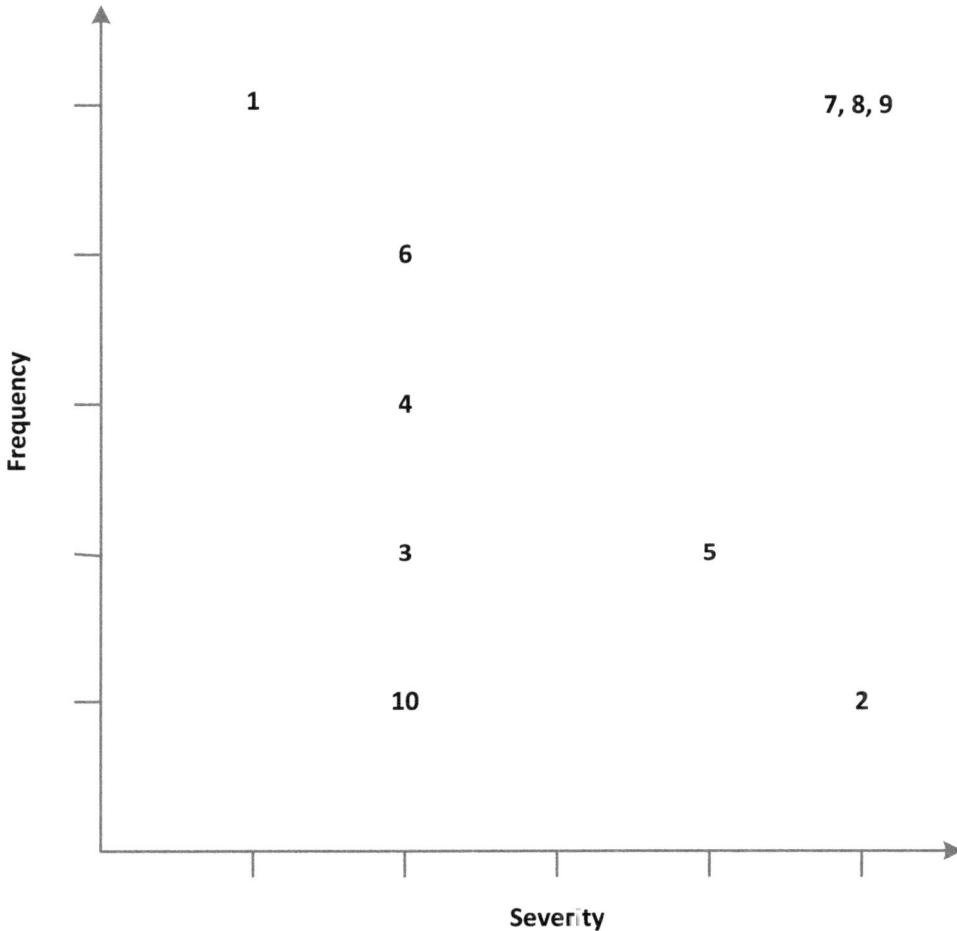

1 = Power outages in Raleigh plant
2 = Hurricane at Birmingham plant
3 = Foreign exchange variability
4 = Equipment failure
5 = Pollution ordinance shutdown

6 = Commodity price swings
7 = Damage to Thailand supplier
8 = Disruption of deliveries by train
9 = Bottleneck staffing shortage
10 = Assembly staff union walkout

The zero-to-five scale used in the sample chart can be clarified in greater detail, so that those people deriving scores for risks can set scores with a fair degree of reliability. For example, the following frequency scoring system sets ranges for each of the scores from zero to five.

Frequency Scoring Guidelines

Score	Description	Time Guideline
5	Frequent activity	Weekly
4	High activity	Quarterly
3	Normal activity	Annually
2	Modest activity	Every 2-3 years
1	Low activity	Every 5+ years
0	No activity	No historical activity whatsoever

The same approach can be applied to the severity of a risk, as described in the following severity scoring system. In the sample scoring guidelines, the table notes multiple ways in which to set a zero-to-five score, since it is not always possible to define a risk based on a single set of criteria.

Severity Scoring Guidelines

Score	Description	Sales Reduction	Expense Increase	Order Fulfillment Rate in 24 Hours
5	Potentially business threatening	Sales terminated	50% increase	0%
4	Major disruption	50% decline	25% increase	50%
3	Concerning to stakeholders	20% decline	10% increase	75%
2	Material impact	10% decline	5% increase	80%
1	Minor impact	5% decline	2% increase	90%
0	No impact	< 1% decline	< 0.5% increase	98%

Note that in the preceding severity scoring guidelines table, the percentages listed for a sales reduction are higher than the percentages used for an expense increase. The reason for the difference is that the effects of a sales reduction are reduced by the cost of goods sold, which will not occur if there is no sale. This means that the severity scoring will vary, depending on the gross margin that a company earns. For example, a potential sales reduction of 10% may be considered to have a material impact if the contribution margin is high, since most of the sale passes through to profits. Conversely, a potential sales reduction of 10% might be considered to have a minor impact if the contribution margin is relatively low, since only a small part of each sale appears in profits.

Risk Quantification Issues

Some risks initially appear so vague that it may not seem possible to assign any value to them at all. For example, what is the cost of the loss of a company's reputation? While certainly difficult, it may be possible to estimate these costs by examining what happened to other companies that experienced the same or similar problems in the past.

Examples of risks that certainly pose quantification difficulties are:

- Losses from a customer boycott
- Reduced sales from a decline in the perception of a brand
- Difficulty in hiring high-grade employees because of a reputational issue

Other risks are considerably easier to quantify, since a specific action should result in a tightly-defined cost. For example, if a factory is located in a flood plain, flooding damage will be limited to the complete replacement of the factory, along with lost profits from sales that could not be fulfilled from that factory. Similarly, asset expropriation can be tightly defined; the assets located in the at-risk country will be taken.

The cost of some risks will fall midway between the two extremes just noted, and may encompass expenditures that a business has not been accustomed to dealing with in the past. For example, a company dealing with a loss in reputation may need to factor in the cost of a lobbyist, extra security personnel to protect company property, a community relations manager, payments to the local populace, an advertising campaign, a public relations advisor, incentive packages to retain or hire employees, and so forth.

Once risks have been quantified, there may be a temptation to multiply the expected cost range by the probability of occurrence, which results in an expected value. For example, if the probability of an event is 10% and the cost of an unfavorable outcome is $1 million, we multiply the cost by the probability to arrive at an expected value of $100,000. The trouble with the expected value concept is that it tends to hide the sheer size of some risks. For example, a risk may have a cost of $100 million but a probability of only ¼%, so anyone examining the expected value report would reasonably conclude that the risk is worth only $250,000. In reality, management should be made aware of the total projected cost of a risk, even if the risk is small, to see which risks are hefty enough to bring down a business. This means that both the probability and cost information for each risk should be disseminated.

The Risk Profile

A risk profile is a categorization of the main risks that can impact an organization. A risk profile document is useful for focusing the attention of management on those risks that can cause significant turmoil for the entity, either in terms of financial losses or operational difficulties. The types of categories used can vary by organization. Here are a number of risk categories that might be used:

- *Brand*. Includes issues that can cause the perception of a company's brand to decline, such as a product recall, a marketing flop, bad publicity, negative product reviews, and public squabbles with business partners.
- *Catastrophic*. Primarily includes natural disasters, such as hurricanes, earthquakes, tornadoes, and floods.
- *Environmental*. Includes fines and remediation costs related to pollution, as well as damage to the environment.

- *Financial.* Includes the risks of customer nonpayment, foreign exchange rate variability, capital availability concerns, and employee fraud.
- *Human resources.* Includes the loss of key employees and the lack of properly directive leadership.
- *Industry risk.* Includes factors that can alter the competitive profile of the industry, such as changes in the entire size of the market that the industry serves, the rate at which the industry is consolidating, and the ability of new competitors to enter the market.
- *Information technology.* Includes factors that do not allow an organization to have responsive IT systems, such as being tied to legacy software and having a significant amount of systems downtime. Can also include system breaches that result in the loss of key data.
- *International.* Includes factors caused by doing business in other countries, such as employee kidnappings, terrorist attacks, asset expropriation, political unrest, and sanctions.
- *Legal and regulatory.* Includes new laws or regulatory requirements, such as changes in available tax credits and increased filing requirements for publicly held companies. Can also include internal legal issues, such as being unable to lock down trade secrets.
- *Operational.* Includes factors that impact the ability to produce a sufficient number of quality goods and services, such as inadequate peak capacity, low fulfillment rates, high scrap rates, and processes not being followed.
- *Strategic.* Includes risks arising from the decisions that management makes to follow certain strategic directions. Examples of these risks are bringing new products too late to market, being unable to secure key distribution channels, and selling a product mix that does not attract a sufficient number of customers.

The risk profile document can be combined with the preceding risk rankings chart to yield a good overview of the risks to which a business is subjected. This report can be used as the basis for risk management planning, budgeting, and presentations to the board of directors and the investment community.

Special Risk Situations

The preceding risk profile is a good way to slot a large number of potential risks into readily identifiable classifications. But what if a number of correlated risks occur at the same time? These "perfect storm" events are quite rare, but *do* happen. The key issue with perfect storm events is that they do not easily fit within a single classification. Instead, there tends to be a general triggering of multiple risks across several classifications that have a major negative impact on an organization – and the trigger is an unanticipated event. For example, a large earthquake hits Haiti, which triggers a tsunami that destroys shore properties all over the Caribbean. An operator of tourist resorts with multiple properties across the Caribbean could be nearly destroyed by such an event. Or, a clothing retailer's five key suppliers are all located in Bangladesh, which suffers catastrophic flooding as part of the annual monsoon season, thereby shutting down all deliveries to the retailer for months.

It can be exceedingly difficult to anticipate perfect storm events, because they are so rare, and may be triggered by events far away from the organization. Nonetheless, there are several ways to spot potential perfect storms, which are:

- *Geographical view.* Create a geographical model of where all company facilities and the facilities of its suppliers and customers are located. Then layer onto this model the natural disasters that can occur in each of these areas, and along the supply lines between the various facilities. This can trigger discussions of possible perfect storm events.
- *Correlation view.* Work through the risk categories listed under the earlier Risk Profile sub-section, and consider the types of triggering events that could impact multiple categories of risk, either at once or in a cascading manner.
- *Historical view.* Work back through a history of the industry for many years to determine what types of events have occurred in the past, no matter how infrequently, and see if any of them could apply to the company's current circumstances, perhaps in a modified form.
- *Complexity view.* Review which company systems are complex and therefore prone to failure, and especially those systems that have a significant impact on the ability of the firm to do business. Also make note of the company's ability to recover when these systems go down. A further consideration is when these complex systems are being operating in a lean manner, which means that there are few resources available to bring them back on line when they fail.

Risks may be ignored or incorrectly considered to have reduced effects when they are spread across or shared with several functional areas of a business. In this situation, the following issues can arise:

- When a risk applies to two or more functional areas, there can be a tendency for the manager of each function to assume that the other manager is responsible for it, so that no risk mitigation activities occur.
- A risk that is considered moderate or minor for one area may be present for several areas; if the risk occurs, it then impacts a broad swathe of the company's functionality, and is more likely to be classified as a major risk.

Both of these issues can be addressed through a heightened level of coordination across the functional areas, which means that risk mitigation requires the cooperation of all company departments.

Risk Planning Timeline

Proper attention to risk management requires that it be attended to on a continuing basis, as the need arises. However, there should also be a more formal annual process, during which risks that have already been identified are reviewed to see if they have changed or if the risk mitigation strategy should be altered. This process can also involve a formal review of the business environment and operations to see if any new risks have arisen. The timeline for this formal review will vary, depending on the size and complexity of a business. The following schedule can be considered a general guideline for planning activities and when they should occur.

Sample Risk Planning Timeline

Week 1	Circulate to the management team the listing of risks identified as part of the last annual planning process, with instructions to judge the current level of severity of these risks and whether they should be dealt with differently in the future.
Week 2	Meet to discuss changes to the existing list of identified risks, which includes a discussion of contemplated changes to the overall business plan. Issue meeting minutes, along with an updated list of identified risks.
Week 3	Meet to discuss mitigation activities to apply to the revised list of identified risks.
Week 4	Analyze the sufficiency and cost of the identified mitigation activities. Release results to the management team.
Week 5	Meet again to discuss whether the initially identified risk mitigation activities are sufficient. If not, revise the stated amount of these activities.
Week 6	Present the revised risk mitigation plan to the board of directors.

Risk Management Best Practices

Over time, the methods that a business uses for dealing with risk likely stultify. There will be an accepted group of improvements that have been in use for a long time, with (at best) a trickle of additional ideas appearing thereafter. This is because the management of risk will appear to have settled into a standard routine, so there will be little apparent need or willingness to find new best practices that can improve the risk management situation. There are several ways to break out of this malaise, which are as follows:

- *Cross-department reviews.* Routinely sponsor a gathering of those individuals in the various departments and subsidiaries who are actively involved in risk management, and have them make presentations to the group regarding their risk management techniques. This is most effective in a silo situation, where risk management is dealt with at the local level, rather than centrally.
- *Benchmarking.* Sponsor visits to other organizations that are dealing with the same risk issues, to learn about their risk management practices.
- *New acquisition reviews.* Whenever the company acquires another business, send in a risk management investigatory team to see if they can unearth any new best practices. This can be particularly effective if the new subsidiary is located in a different industry, where there may be entirely different risk management practices.

- *Risk log analysis*. Whenever a significant risk-related loss occurs, log it into a database that tracks risk events. Then bring up the issue before the risk management committee, and hire a risk management consultant to attend. This is an ideal situation in which to bring in consultants, since they can provide advice regarding the solutions they have found elsewhere that can mitigate the risk that is under review. A risk log can also be used to identify recurring risks that, if not addressed, could eventually cause a major problem for the business.

As risk management best practices are found through any of the preceding methods, log them into a database of best practices, and make it available throughout the organization. The CRO can be particularly effective in publicizing this database and advocating the use of newly unearthed best practices.

The best way to drive risk management best practices down through an organization is to create a series of training sessions that discuss business processes, where problems are likely to be encountered, and how to address them. This approach is particularly effective if the trainers incorporate case studies into the discussions that involve events that have occurred within the firm. These sessions can be updated to incorporate the latest best practices that have been discovered through the preceding list of activities.

Risk Management Themes

There are several general themes that well-managed businesses usually follow, and which keep them from adopting risky behavior patterns. If the management team adheres to the following concepts, it is much less likely to experience major losses or participate in highly risky, high-return enterprises. These themes are:

- *Deep knowledge of the business*. Risky behavior is much less likely to arise when every employee of a business has a deep knowledge of his or her own responsibilities, and also how the organization as a whole operates. When there is a well-trained work force, many more people can spot anomalies that may lead to losses, and will also recognize the associated risks that accompany new business proposals This level of detailed knowledge should cover absolutely everyone – from the board of directors down to production-line employees. This level of knowledge can only be obtained through the long-term training of all employees on all aspects of the business. It also requires basic business policies to promote employee retention, such as excellent benefits, a commitment to retain staff during business downturns, and promoting from within.

EXAMPLE

Creekside Industrial hires a hot new prospect into the purchasing department who comes from a leading university, and who wants to experiment with many new ways to save money for the company. One of her proposals is to use hedging strategies to mitigate swings in the costs of several metals that Creekside uses in its production processes. The idea is interesting, but no one else in the business has any experience with the hedging concept. What steps should Mr. Haley, the purchasing manager, take?

Creekside has had a long-term commitment to ensuring that there is a thorough understanding of every aspect of its business. Since hedging is entirely new, Mr. Haley takes the following steps to reduce the associated risk of hedging:

1. Discusses the matter with the risk management committee and gains their preliminary approval of the concept.
2. Hires a consulting firm to make presentations to the board of directors, risk management committee, and purchasing department regarding the mechanics of the hedging process and the risks that can arise.
3. Retains the consulting firm to engage in a small number of hedging transactions on a pilot basis, instructing the purchasing staff about the process. This includes creating policies and procedures.
4. The consulting firm then switches roles and oversees several purchasing employees as they engage in more hedging transactions and provides corrective advice as needed.
5. The internal audit department is brought in and examines the proposed process flow. The internal audit manager devises several audit procedures that will be conducted periodically to ensure that the hedging process is operating as planned. The external auditors are notified of the hedging initiative and examine the initial process flow, as well as the internal audit team's proposed examination plans. The external auditors provide advice regarding any issues found.
6. The risk management committee and then the board of directors give their formal approval of the hedging activity, and both request an initial quarterly milestone review meeting to discuss the outcome of initial hedging activities.
7. Hedging activities begin.

Mr. Haley has acted correctly in bringing numerous parties into the discussion of a hedging initiative, while also obtaining expert advice from a third party. He then ensures that the hedging activities are properly described and monitored, and that many people both inside and outside of the purchasing department are made aware of this activity.

The worst action that Mr. Haley could have taken would be to allow the new hire to solely pursue the hedging concept, which would have the dual negative effects of concentrating knowledge of the process with one person, and of creating the risk of an incorrect hedge that might be mistakenly entered into because the individual has no direct experience in hedging transactions.

- *Infrastructure commitment.* A proper level of risk management requires deep controls in selected parts of an organization – even if those controls are expensive and/or interfere with the efficient processing of transactions. In a business that focuses excessively on streamlining operations and cutting out costs, it is likely that key controls will be removed, thereby making it more likely that high-loss incidents will occur. This issue is less likely when responsibility over processes and controls is kept away from profit center managers, so there is no temptation to reduce controls in order to increase profits. A strong commitment to infrastructure is especially important when there is a drive to re-engineer processes, since the newly reformulated systems are likely to contain fewer controls than the predecessor systems.

EXAMPLE

Celsius Corporation is under significant cost pressure, so the management team has elected to centralize all accounting operations into one location, rather than the current situation, where all four company subsidiaries employ their own accounting departments. The change is expected to yield annual cost savings of $4,000,000, due to reduced headcount and being able to pay software maintenance fees on a single accounting software package.

The projected cost savings are so attractive that the senior management team is pushing for a quick rollout of the new, centralized operation. However, the controller is concerned that the wholesale shutdown of accounting systems will result in key controls being deleted. She asks the internal audit manager to investigate the situation, which results in the following findings:

- The new system has no provision for having local supervisors manually approve employee overtime at the subsidiaries, which presents the risk that overtime will be fraudulently claimed.
- The new system has no provision for comparing supplier invoices to receipt records (which are maintained locally), so there is a risk that false or excessively large supplier invoices will be paid.
- The new system automatically sends electronic invoices to customers, with no provision for a manual proofreading step, as had previously been the case. The company issues extremely complex invoices to its customers, so proofreading is needed to keep customers from rejecting invoices.

The findings are included in the implementation plan for the new system. In addition, the controller asks the internal audit manager to schedule a series of reviews of all aspects of the new system, to see if any other issues arise from the loss of controls.

- *Activity boundaries*. Many business transactions can be taken to excess, so it is necessary to set boundaries to limit them. For example, it may be acceptable to write 1,000 insurance policies for flood damage in Louisiana, but writing 100,000 of them will expose an insurer to a potentially massive loss if the Mississippi River overflows its banks. Similarly, it may be unwise to double the amount of credit available to a customer, if the amount of this increase would expose the seller to a large enough bad debt to destroy the business.

EXAMPLE

The president of Henderson Industrial has retired, so the board of directors conducts a search and hires an outsider, Mr. Blinker. The new president negotiates for an expanded range of authority, which gives him a high level of overriding control over the entire business, with few checks and balances.

After a few months, the chief risk officer notes a number of circumstances in which controls have been overridden by Mr. Blinker, which were specifically allowed when his three-year contract was negotiated. Specifically, he has mandated increased production levels and then offered promotions to distributors to buy goods now. He has also offered much longer payment terms to key customers, and is planning an expansion into a country that all of Henderson's competitors have abandoned due to the level of unrest in that region. Mr. Blinker's reasoning in taking these steps is to boost sales. However, the added sales come at the risk of higher returns from distributors, more bad debts from customers, and outright business failure in the new sales region. In short, the president is accepting much more risk in exchange for increased sales. The risk levels taken on all of these activities exceed the boundaries set by his predecessor, who advocated no channel stuffing, reasonable payment terms, and no foreign sales activity.

The chief risk officer takes his concerns to the audit committee, which brings the matter to the attention of the board of directors. Shortly thereafter, the company issues a press release that Mr. Blinker is leaving the company to pursue other interests.

- *Performance targets.* The management team should set reasonable performance targets for a business. By doing so, employees can set a reasonable and sustainable annual pace at which to grow sales. If targets are set too high, and especially if compensation systems match the high targets, then expect employees to engage in increasingly risky behavior, if not outright fraud, in order to meet the imposed targets. The performance targets to be set depend on the stage in the life of a product or business. Early sales may increase at a prodigious growth rate until the market reaches maturity, at which point vastly lower performance targets should be set. This is also a function of the gross sales level of a business – that is, an organization with $1 million in sales may reasonably expect to double its sales in one year, but a $10 billion business is extremely unlikely to duplicate this feat.

EXAMPLE

Medusa Medical sells a special blend of rapeseed oil through retail stores that specialize in home health care products. Since its founding four years before, the company has experienced 50% average annual sales growth. A venture capital fund has invested several million dollars in the company, in the belief that the business can grow at an even faster rate.

To meet the inflated sales figures that the founder used to attract the venture capitalists, the sales target for the next year is set at a level 80% higher than the year before. To achieve this goal, the company hires an appropriate number of sales representatives, but does not plan on an adequate ramp up period in which to train the new hires. Also, there is an incorrect assumption that additional sales can be squeezed from the existing sales regions, which proves not to be the case. As a result, all of the new hires find that they are falling far behind their sales quotas, and so resort to making sales pitches to financially questionable retailers. The resulting orders trigger a much higher level of bad debt losses than the company had experienced in the past. At year-end, sales do not reach the anticipated levels, while profits actually decline due to the extra costs of the new hires and bad debts.

EXAMPLE

In the past year, the price of oil increased to an all-time high, so the senior management team of Franklin Drilling decided to implement a new bonus plan that compensates the entire management team based on the number of new wells drilled from which there is a minimum threshold amount of oil flow per day. The intent is to greatly increase the volume of oil that Franklin can sell in the next year, presumably reaping massive profits. The company plans to invest an average of $2.5 million in each hole drilled.

Seeing massive bonuses in their future, the management group enthusiastically leases land in prime drilling areas and invests in the drilling of dozens of wells. In the meantime, the price of oil plummets. However, the management team continues to drill, since their incentive plan does not account for changes in the price of oil – they are only interested in producing more oil. By the end of the year, the company has invested over $100 million in new wells and $5 million in bonus payouts, but is forced to cap many of the wells, because the market price of oil now makes it unprofitable to extract the oil.

A better approach would have been to tie overall performance to profitability, since doing so would have accounted for variations in the market price of oil.

Biases in Risk Management

Throughout this book, we assume that individuals will take a balanced view of the available information and use it to derive a well-considered set of risk management actions. However, the decisions (or non-decisions) that people take do not always match these expectations. Instead, the outcomes may be substantially worse than one might expect. There are a number of reasons why risk management actions do not always appear to be prudent, including the following:

- *The blindness of familiarity*. Managers may feel comfortable with the current operating situation, because they deal with it every day. During their time on the job, they may never have experienced a disaster, and therefore assume that disasters do not occur. This is an incorrect belief – disasters merely occur so infrequently that managers have not yet experienced one. In this situation, a person is more inclined to make no provision to guard against a worse outcome, primarily due to his or her excessive degree of familiarity with the environment.
- *Excessive focus on a goal*. The management team may have a powerful financial incentive to achieve a specific goal, perhaps a profit number that will yield a major bonus payoff for them. If so, they may be willing to do *anything* to achieve their goal, including continuing to pursue that goal even when the available evidence indicates that they will not reach it. For example, a profit goal is clearly out of reach in the fourth quarter, so the management team speculates in derivatives to obtain their goal – despite the low probability of achieving success.

- *The group opinion.* Managers may rely upon each other's opinions in making decisions, rather than inspecting the hard data in detail. This tendency to form a group opinion causes the biases of managers to have an undue influence on the risk management decisions made. This is a particular problem when there is a strong opinion leader in the group, whose views tend to sway everyone else. This is a common problem when the founders and CEOs of businesses exercise an excessive amount of power.

It is quite difficult for managers to see any of these effects while decisions are being made, perhaps because this is the normal way of reaching decisions within an organization. It may require the analysis of an outsider to point out what has happened, and the negative effects it has had on risk management decisions.

Summary

The development of a system that truly manages risk is not one that only deals with the most obvious risks; and it is not one that continually copies forward the plan from the preceding year. Instead, a high-grade risk management plan is the result of a thoughtful process that continually reexamines a business and its environment, with a particular focus on any changes that may alter the risk profile of the entity. Further, the risk management mindset should be driven deep into the fundamentals of the business, so that it is routinely considered as part of many business decisions.

A risk management mindset is not intended to destroy the entrepreneurial spirit of a company. There must always be a willingness to take risks in the pursuit of a new market or the release of a new product. However, employees must be made aware of the risk implications of their actions, so that they can make properly balanced judgments about what to do.

In the following chapters, we address risk management issues related to specific functional areas of an organization.

Chapter 2
Treasury Risk Management

Introduction

When people think about risk management, they probably consider treasury issues first. This part of a business contains a multitude of major risks related to funding, credit, investments, liquidity, foreign exchange, and interest rates. Some financially-oriented organizations consider treasury to be the *only* significant source of serious risk in their business models.

Treasury risks are considered so important because they can cause large losses and eliminate cash reserves within a short period of time, possibly resulting in bankruptcy. At a minimum, treasury risk can cause wild fluctuations in earnings that interfere with the planning processes of a firm. Given the seriousness of these issues, we spend far longer in the following sections discussing the risks of this functional area than any other part of a business.

Funding Risk

A major concern with any corporate expansion is when the strategy calls for funding, and the treasurer cannot raise the money. This is particularly common in a tight credit market, where there is nothing fundamentally wrong with the company's creditworthiness. Instead, funds are simply not available. Here are several risk mitigation options:

- *Adopt a longer-term debt mix.* When funds are available in a looser credit market, obtain more long-term debt than the company actually needs. This could involve a mix of bank loans of medium-term duration and bonds that have a lengthy maturity. Doing so builds a cash reserve that can be accessed whenever needed for years to come.
- *Sweeten debt with equity instruments.* Offer convertible debt to investors. For example, a bond might have attached warrants, where the warrant exercise price is set low enough to be tempting to investors. In this case, investors will be more likely to buy the bonds, irrespective of the state of the credit market.
- *Adopt a DRIP plan.* If the company routinely pays dividends to its investors, offer a dividend reinvestment plan (DRIP) to investors, where the company can use their dividend payments to automatically purchase additional shares of company stock. Doing so diverts dividend payments straight back into the company's coffers. This is not an overly large source of funding.
- *Adopt an employee stock purchase plan.* Offer employees the opportunity to buy the company's stock at a modest discount from the market price. Payments are typically taken from employee paychecks as a standard deduction,

so that stock purchases tend to run for a long period of time. This generally results in a relatively small amount of additional funding for the company.

- *Work with several lenders.* Have long-term lending arrangements with multiple lenders. By doing so, the company still has an established relationship with at least one lender if its main lender decides to cut off any further funding. This is not necessarily an easy tactic to follow, since the primary lender will try to maximize its profits by forcing the company to borrow solely from it.

An additional consideration when dealing with funding risk is how much cash a business should keep on hand to guard against unexpected losses. In a relatively staid business where cash flows are highly predictable and risks are intentionally kept low, there may be little need for a reserve of cash. However, an organization that has highly variable cash flows and a large appetite for risk may need to maintain substantial funding reserves. The concept of "funding reserves" does not necessarily mean maintaining a cash balance. A company could have little cash on hand but a large untapped line of credit that gives it significant funding reserves.

To expand upon the concept of a funding reserve, the management team may target having quite a high credit rating, which may be critical if it plans to engage in substantial borrowings and needs to acquire debt at the lowest possible interest rate. In this situation, the credit rating agency will only award a high credit rating if a business has a massive cash reserve (not just a large amount of available debt). A large cash balance allows an organization to absorb a number of large losses, and makes its debt instruments a safe investment. Conversely, if management is comfortable with a lower credit rating, it can maintain much lower cash reserves.

Investment Risk

An entity may invest in instruments that yield high returns, but at the price of having a high risk of loss, as well. For example, a treasurer who is focusing on high returns might invest in a derivative instrument as an investment strategy, rather than as a hedging strategy. If so, the treasurer is taking the position of a speculator, hoping that a positive return will materialize. The resulting loss could be massive.

Investment risk frequently arises from the incentives and restrictions (if any) placed on the treasury department. For example, if a bonus plan will pay the treasury staff for achieving a high return on investment, then speculation-grade investments can only be expected. A better approach is to deliberately downgrade the need to achieve a return on investment, and instead use investment policies to orient the department toward safe investments that are easily convertible into cash. A sample investment policy follows.

SAMPLE INVESTMENT POLICY

General

Investments in securities with low liquidity levels shall be restricted to 15% of the company's total investment portfolio. There must be an active secondary market for all other investments.

Debt Investments

Debt investments are subject to the following restrictions:

- May only be made in high-quality intermediate or long-term corporate and Treasury bonds
- No more than 20% of the total debt investment can be made in a single industry
- Investments cannot comprise more than 5% of the debt issuances of the investee
- The average term to maturity cannot exceed __ years
- An investment must be terminated within one month if its Standard & Poor's credit rating drops below BBB
- Any bank acting as a counterparty shall have a capital account of at least $5 billion
- Short-term investments shall be pre-qualified by the investment advisory committee for the placement of funds

Equity Investments

Equity investments are subject to the following restrictions:

- May only be made in the common stock of companies trading on the New York Stock Exchange
- No more than 20% of the total equity investment can be made in a single industry
- Investments cannot comprise more than 5% of the capitalization of the investee

Prohibitions

The company is prohibited from investing in any of the following types of investments without the prior approval of the board of directors:

- Commodities
- Foreign equity investments and commercial paper
- Leveraged transactions
- Real estate
- Securities with junk ratings
- Short sales or purchases on margin
- Venture capital

Liquidity Risk

A company may have a large amount of cash invested, but a large part of the cash is locked into long-term investments. If so, the cash will not be available for use if there is a sudden short-term need for cash, which can trigger quite a scramble to locate funding that can be used at once. The following investment activities can mitigate this liquidity risk:

- *Prioritize investment criteria*. The business can specifically emphasize in its investment policy the need to have immediate liquidity for most or all of its investments. It is useful to also downplay any emphasis on achieving a high return on investment, since a high return usually requires a longer-term investment period.
- *Match maturities*. An option requiring manual tracking is to match the maturities of investments to when the cash will be needed for operational purposes. This method calls for a highly accurate cash forecast, both in terms of the amounts and timing of cash flows. To be safe, maturities can be planned for several days prior to a forecasted cash need, though this reduces the return on investment.
- *Tiered investments*. If a business has more cash than it needs for ongoing operational requirements, the treasury staff can conduct an analysis to determine how much cash is never or rarely required for operations, and use this cash in a more aggressive investment strategy. For example:
  - *Continual cash usage*. Cash usage levels routinely flow within a certain range, so there must be sufficient cash available to always meet these cash requirements. The investment strategy for the amount included in this investment tier should be concentrated in highly liquid investments that can be readily accessed, with less attention to achieving a high rate of return.
  - *Occasional cash usage*. In addition to cash usage for daily operating events, there are usually a small number of higher cash usage events that can be readily predicted, such as a periodic income tax or dividend payment. The strategy for this investment tier should focus on maturity dates just prior the scheduled usage of cash, along with a somewhat greater emphasis on the return on investment. There should be a secondary market for these types of investments.
  - *No planned cash usage*. If cash usage levels have never exceeded a certain amount, all cash above this maximum usage level can be invested in longer-term instruments that have higher returns on investment, and perhaps with more limited secondary markets.

EXAMPLE

The treasurer of Suture Corporation wants to adopt a tiered investment strategy. He finds that the company routinely requires a maximum of $200,000 of cash for various expenditures on a weekly basis. In addition, there are scheduled quarterly dividend payments of $50,000 per quarter, and quarterly income tax payments of $100,000, which fall on the same date. There have not been any instances in the past three years where cash requirements exceeded these amounts. Currently, Suture maintains cash reserves of $850,000 on a weekly basis. Based on the preceding information, the company could invest the cash in the following ways:

Investment Tier	Amount	Investment Type
Continual cash usage	$200,000	Money market
Occasional cash usage	150,000	Certificates of deposit, commercial paper
No planned cash usage	500,000	Bonds
Total	$850,000	

The tiered investment strategy requires close attention to the cash forecast, particularly in regard to the timing and amount of the occasional cash usage items. Otherwise, there is a risk of being caught with too much cash in an illiquid investment when there is an immediate need for the cash, so a risk mitigation strategy might emphasize minimizing or even eliminating the classification for no planned cash usage.

Credit Policy Risk

The corporate strategy may call for a loosening of credit terms in order to attract additional customers, and/or more orders from existing customers. For example, credit terms may be extended from net 15 days to net 60 days. If so, this represents a substantial increase in the amount of funding that will be required to support accounts receivable. If the company does not have the requisite amount of cash, the treasurer will be forced to look outside the company for more funding, which may not be available.

Another type of credit policy risk arises when the policy is not altered rapidly enough to account for changes in the financial condition of customers. For example, if there is a decline in general economic conditions, there may be a higher incidence of bankruptcy among customers, or at least longer days outstanding for receivables. This increased risk of bad debt losses and/or larger investment in working capital could have been reduced or eliminated if the credit policy were more frequently updated to match conditions.

Credit Exposure Risk

Even if a business routinely updates its credit policy and correctly enforces it, there is a risk that certain customers will unexpectedly be unable to pay their bills at all, resulting in bad debts. A certain number of bad debts are an expected part of doing business, and a reserve is created against the expectation of these occurrences. However, there is the risk that a large customer will suddenly and unexpectedly go out of business and be unable to pay its debts. This is a particular problem when a company gains most of its sales from a small number of large customers. There are several possible solutions, as outlined in the following sub-sections.

Internal Credit Rating System

It is possible to develop an internal credit rating system, since the credit staff has access to a large amount of information about customers, especially those that have been doing business with the company for a long time. An internal credit rating system should be based on any factors that a company finds to be important in determining the credit quality of customers in its specific industry. It is entirely possible that a credit determinant of ability to pay in one industry is a relatively minor one in another industry. Thus, the mix and weightings given to factors in the home improvement industry for contractor customers may differ wildly from those used by a sporting goods manufacturer for its retailer customers. Despite the broad potential range of variability in factors, the following are considered to be among the more reliable indicators of creditworthiness:

- *Bankruptcy*. There should not have been a recent bankruptcy filing, or the prospect of one.
- *Legal proceedings*. There should be no tax liens or other judgments against the customer.
- *Liquidity*. The customer's current assets greatly exceed its current liabilities, as measured by the current ratio or quick ratio.
- *Payment history*. The customer should have a track record of reliably paying on time.
- *Profitability*. The customer has a history of achieving a profit over the past few years, preferably close to the median profit level for the industry.
- *Stability*. The longer the customer has been in business, the better.
- *Third party credit score*. The credit score assigned to the customer by a credit scoring business should indicate that it is a reliable payer to *all* of its suppliers.

To construct an internal credit rating system, itemize the factors to be used in the system, and assign a range of scores to each of the factors that are either added to or subtracted from a customer's score. The following table illustrates the concept.

Point Assignment for Credit Scoring

Credit Scoring Factor	Excellent	Average	Neutral	Poor
Liquidity	+10	+5	-5	-10
Profitability	+15	+5	-5	-15
Payment history	+20	+5	0	-10
Stability	+5	0	-10	-20
Adverse judgments	0	0	0	-20
Third party credit score	+10	0	-5	-10
Bankruptcy	0	0	0	-100

The scores assigned in the preceding table can vary substantially, depending on the company's experience with how a particular factor appears to impact the ability of a customer to pay in a timely manner. For example, the credit manager may decide that payment history is the most important factor, and so assigns a large number of points to an excellent rating for that factor.

Also, note how some scores in the point assignment table are only activated if there is a negative result. Thus, there are only large negative scores related to bankruptcy or adverse judgments; a customer is not awarded points for the absence of these factors.

The point scoring system should be designed to keep a large cluster of customers from inhabiting the high and low ends of the scoring range. It is not useful when the assigned scores indicate that all customers should be granted maximum credit, or that none of them deserve credit, since this does not provide useful information.

The points assigned under a credit scoring system can be used as thresholds for a variety of actions by the credit staff. For example, a score of 60 or more may allow for the automatic granting of credit, while a score between 40 and 50 calls for an escalated review, and scores between 30 and 40 indicate the need for a personal guarantee.

EXAMPLE

The credit manager of Kelvin Corporation is evaluating the credit application of a prospective new customer, which has submitted a complete set of audited financial statements. Further investigation reveals that the applicant has a 3:1 quick ratio, has been solidly profitable for the past five years, and has no adverse judgments against it. The business has been assigned an average credit score by a third party scoring firm. Based on this information, the credit manager assigns the following score to the applicant:

Factor	Issues	Score
Liquidity	High liquidity level	+10
Profitability	High historical profitability	+15
Stability	Five year history	+5
Adverse judgments	None detected	0
Third party credit score	Average ranking	<u>0</u>
	Score	<u>+30</u>

In essence, the ranking indicates that the applicant is an ideal prospective customer. According to Kelvin's credit policy, the applicant should be offered a $10,000 initial maximum credit, with re-evaluation to occur once a payment history has been compiled over the next six months. If the payment history is acceptable, the applicant can then be assigned an additional ten points, which will give it a total credit score of 40 and allow the credit manager to increase its maximum credit to $25,000.

A number of additional features can be applied to an internal credit scoring system that may enhance its usefulness. Consider the following features:

- Adjust credit scores based on the economic environment, where (for example) a contracting economy results in an automatic 5% reduction in all credit scores, thereby contracting the total amount of credit offered.
- Adjust the credit score based on the average or trending number of days past terms that a customer pays, either with the company or according to a third party credit report.
- Cap the amount of credit granted at a certain percentage of the reported net worth of the applicant.
- Cap the amount of credit granted at the amount of credit granted by anyone else to that customer, as stated on the third party credit report.
- Reduce the credit score of a customer located in a country that is perceived to have a high level of political risk.
- Reduce a credit score an increasing amount based on how long the applicant has been unable to report a profit.
- Reduce the number of points assigned to an applicant if its financial statements have not been audited, thereby reflecting the increased unreliability of the underlying information.

Third Party Credit Ratings

A business may find that it has too few customers to develop a sufficient pool of information for its own in-house credit rating system. Also, it may not compile enough information about its customers to develop a rating system. If so, a common option is to subscribe to a third party credit rating service. Even a business that has an internal credit rating system may buy such a subscription in order to supplement its own system.

A credit rating organization, such as Experian or Dun & Bradstreet, collects information from many customers about their credit experiences with other entities, and also collects public information about liens, bankruptcies, and so forth, and aggregates this information into a credit report. These credit reports can be purchased with varying amounts of information, such as a credit rating, payment performance trend, legal filings, corporate officers, and much more.

The credit rating assigned to a business is based on the credit scoring methodology developed by the credit rating organization, which uses certain types of information and applies weightings that may differ from what a company would use if it were to develop its own credit scores. Nonetheless, these third party credit scores can provide a valuable view of how outside scoring analysts calculate credit scores.

> **Tip:** If a credit reporting subscription is purchased, be sure to include automatic updates of major changes in customer status, so that notifications of large credit downgrades or bankruptcies are received by e-mail as soon as possible.

Credit Insurance

It may be possible to shift some credit exposure risk to a firm that provides credit insurance. Under a credit insurance policy, the insurer protects the seller against customer nonpayment. The insurer should be willing to provide coverage against customer nonpayment if a proposed customer clears its internal review process.

As is the case with all insurance policies, be sure to examine the terms of a credit insurance agreement for exclusions, to see what the insurer will not cover. In particular, coverage should include the receivables of customers that file for bankruptcy protection or simply go out of business.

Insurers will only provide coverage for legally sustainable debts, which are those receivables that are not disputed by the customer. If there is a dispute, the insurer will only provide coverage after the company has won a court judgment against the customer. The issue of a legally sustainable debt can be a serious one if a company has a track record of disputes with its customers over product quality, damaged goods, returns, and so forth.

> **Tip:** It may be possible to offload the cost of credit insurance to customers by adding it to customer invoices. This is most likely to be acceptable for international deals, where a customer would otherwise be forced to obtain a letter of credit to pay for a transaction.

Insurers are more willing to provide coverage of accounts receivable if the seller is willing to take on a small part of the credit exposure itself. This typically means that a customer default will result in the insurer reimbursing the seller, minus the amount of a 5% to 20% deductible. There may also be an annual aggregate deductible that requires the company to absorb a certain fixed amount of losses in a year before the insurer begins to pay reimbursements. Requiring a deductible means that the company continues to have an interest in only selling to credit-worthy customers.

EXAMPLE

Micron Metallic sells stamping machines to a variety of industrial customers. The company's credit insurance policy states that Micron will absorb the first $200,000 of bad debt losses in each calendar year, after which the insurer will pay 85% of all bad debts incurred, other than for invoices related to international sales, which are not covered by the policy. The policy also specifically excludes receivables related to ABC Company, which the insurer considers to be at an excessively high risk of default.

For some customers, or geographic regions subject to significant political risk, a credit insurer may consider the risk to be so great that it will not provide coverage, or only at a high premium. If so, the credit manager must decide whether it is better for the company to assume the risk of these sales, or to pay the cost of the insurance to obtain coverage. Also, if the insurer discovers that the company's historical loss experience with its customers has been excessively high, it may require such a large premium that the company may conclude that insurance coverage is not a cost-effective form of risk reduction.

Insurers may only be willing to insure a certain amount of receivables per year with some customers. If the company chooses to sell additional amounts on credit to these designated customers, the company will sustain the entire incremental amount of bad debt risk. To avoid the additional risk, it is necessary to track the cumulative amount of credit sales to these customers on an ongoing basis.

Terms Alterations

There may be situations where customers are less able to pay the company's bills in a timely manner, resulting in the credit manager reducing their available credit or even requiring them to pay in advance or on delivery. Here are several ways in which the credit manager can remain satisfied with the credit exposure risk that the company is undertaking, while still allowing the sales department to generate sales:

- *Find alternate payer.* Someone besides the customer agrees to also be liable for payments. This may involve a personal guarantee by the owner or a corporate guarantee that is extended by the corporate parent of the customer. It is sometimes possible to obtain a guarantee from a third party. This may be a related party that has an interest in the operations of the buyer, such as a member of its board of directors, a key supplier, a manager, or a family member. This type of guarantee can be quite valuable, since the assets of the third party may not be so closely tied to the fortunes of the buyer, and can survive the demise of the business.
- *Retain ownership.* It is possible to retain title to goods that are shipped to customers, and only transfer the title to buyers once payment has been made. This can be an effective risk reduction tool, but only if capital goods are being sold – the option is not practical for small-value items.
- *Pay early.* Require the acceleration of payment by customers, so that only smaller payments are at risk of default, and for shorter periods. For example,

a customer requests $30,000 of credit on 30-day payment terms. The credit manager could instead offer $15,000 of credit on 15-day payment terms, which effectively reduces the risk of the company while still giving the customer the same amount of credit over a 30-day period.

Receivables Financing

When management concludes that the credit exposure being undertaken by the organization is too great, it could use a factoring arrangement to transfer the risk to a lender.

Under a factoring arrangement, a finance company agrees to take over a company's accounts receivable collections and keep the money from these collections in exchange for an immediate cash payment to the company. This process typically involves having customers mail their payments to a lockbox that appears to be operated by the company, but which is actually controlled by the finance company. Under a true factoring arrangement, the finance company takes over the risk of loss on any bad debts, though it will have the right to pick which types of receivables it will accept in order to reduce its risk of loss. A finance company is more interested in this type of deal when the size of each receivable is fairly large, since this reduces its per-transaction cost of collection.

If each receivable is quite small, the finance company may still be interested in a factoring arrangement, but it will charge the company extra for its increased processing work. The lender charges an interest rate, as well as a transaction fee for the processing of each invoice it receives. A company working under this arrangement can be paid by the factor at once, or can wait until the invoice due date before payment is sent.

Factoring can be considered a form of financing, since it accelerates the receipt of cash, but it is also a form of risk reduction, since the risk of nonpayment is accepted by the factor. However, the cost of factoring is quite high, making this a less cost-effective option, and probably not a practical one for a business whose margins are already small.

Outside Financing

When the goods being sold are high-cost fixed assets, it may be possible to arrange with a third-party lender to provide financing to the buyer to either buy or lease the items being sold. This type of arrangement shifts the credit risk to the lender. Of course, the lender will apply its own credit granting standards to buyers, and may not provide financing to those customers it considers being at an elevated risk of default.

Portfolio Approach to Risk

Thus far, we have discussed a variety of separate methods that can be used to reduce credit exposure risk. Another option is to summarize the total credit risk to which the business is exposed, and make a determination regarding how much risk to retain. For example, receivables can be categorized into some variation on low, medium, and high risk of nonpayment, and the estimated bad debt percentage calculated for each of these categories. If the total amount of expected bad debt is equal to or less than the amount that management considers to be acceptable, then the current portfolio of risk reduction techniques may be considered acceptable. This means that the credit manager may allow a certain number of higher-risk sales to proceed without risk reduction, as long as there are a large number of extremely low-risk transactions that sufficiently reduce the total credit risk for the company.

EXAMPLE

The credit manager of Laid Back Corporation (which sells business chairs) constructs the following table of estimated bad debts for the company's current portfolio of receivables. The management team has decided that bad debts can reach as much as 1½% of sales. Since the table indicates an expected bad debt percentage of 1.4%, the credit manager has a small amount of room to offer somewhat more credit to higher-risk customers and still remain within the guideline set by management.

Risk Category	Current Receivable Balance	Historical Bad Debt Percentage	Estimated Bad Debt by Risk Category
Low risk	$10,425,000	0.4%	$41,700
Medium low	6,100,000	1.3%	79,300
Medium high	2,350,000	3.8%	89,300
High risk	630,000	10.5%	66,150
Totals	$19,505,000	1.4%	$276,450

The portfolio approach to risk tends to increase earnings, as long as it is used judiciously, since the credit risk associated with customer orders is no longer assessed on an individual basis, but rather as a group of orders where some orders have a higher risk than others.

Cross-Selling Credit Exposure Risk

When a company has multiple lines of business, there is a natural temptation to try to cross-sell the customers of one set of products on the other lines of business. After all, the company has already expended a substantial amount to acquire the customers, and cross-selling is considered to be a relatively inexpensive way to generate additional sales. The trouble with this approach is that a portion of the customers subjected to cross-selling were not good customers to begin with, and their negative impact on the company is now multiplied by their additional purchases. This can have a profound impact on credit exposure risk and company profitability.

Credit exposure risk increases for this subset of customers if they are permitted additional credit. This is a common occurrence that is driven by the sales staff, under the obvious logic that cross-selling will not work unless sales are allowed to increase by providing more credit. The trouble is that the financial position of these customers does not permit them to make additional purchases, resulting in an inevitable increase in payment defaults.

In addition to this credit problem, the expansion of sales to these more difficult customers will also result in more returned goods and more administrative staff time to service their needs. These factors add up to an increase in expenses that, in total, completely offsets any increase in revenues.

The clear answer to the cross-selling conundrum is to carefully analyze all customers prior to initiating a cross-selling campaign, and to exclude the more problematic ones from the campaign. The analysis may even result in the termination of *all* business with these marginal customers.

Credit Concentration Risk

One of the most pervasive credit-related risks relates to the concentration of customers within a single industry. If there is a downturn within an entire industry, then a seller of goods and services into that industry could face a major increase in the number of customers that cannot pay their bills. In essence, the fortunes of the seller are inextricably tied to the welfare of a specific industry.

Many organizations are built around the idea of servicing one industry, so managers cannot see a way out of this type of risk – and there may not be one, if the strategy of the business is to continue servicing one industry. However, there may be opportunities to branch out into adjacent industries that do not suffer from the same economic factors. If so, sales to these other markets may buoy the sales of the business during those periods when the core market is stagnating.

Another way to deal with credit concentration risk is to deliberately acquire unrelated businesses, on the theory that a wide range of markets will eliminate this risk. While concentration risk may indeed be reduced, this approach will generate other issues, such as the inability to manage a diverse portfolio of businesses.

Foreign Exchange Risk Overview

There are several types of foreign exchange risks that can impact a company, and which are described below.

A company may incur *transaction exposure*, which is derived from changes in foreign exchange rates between the dates when a transaction is booked and when it is settled. For example, a company in the United States may sell goods to a company in the United Kingdom, to be paid in pounds having a value at the booking date of $100,000. Later, when the customer pays the company, the exchange rate has changed, resulting in a payment in pounds that translates to a $95,000 sale. Thus, the foreign exchange rate change related to a transaction has created a $5,000 loss for the seller. The following table shows the impact of transaction exposure on different scenarios.

Risk When Transactions Denominated in Foreign Currency

	Import Goods	Export Goods
Home currency weakens	Loss	Gain
Home currency strengthens	Gain	Loss

When a company has foreign subsidiaries, it denominates the recorded amount of their assets and liabilities in the currency of the country in which the subsidiaries generate and expend cash. This *functional currency* is typically the local currency of the country in which a subsidiary operates. When the company reports its consolidated results, it converts these valuations to the home currency of the parent company, which may suffer a loss if exchange rates have declined from the last time when the financial statements were consolidated. This type of risk is known as *translation exposure.*

EXAMPLE

Hammer Industries has a subsidiary located in England, which has its net assets denominated in pounds. The home currency of Hammer is U.S. dollars. At year-end, when the parent company consolidates the financial statements of its subsidiaries, the U.S. dollar has depreciated in comparison to the pound, resulting in a decline in the value of the subsidiary's net assets.

The following table shows the impact of translation exposure on different scenarios.

Risk When Net Assets Denominated in Foreign Currency

	Assets	Liabilities
Home currency weakens	Gain	Loss
Home currency strengthens	Loss	Gain

There are also several types of economic risk related to the specific country within which a company chooses to do business. These risks include:

- *Convertibility risk* is the inability to convert a local currency into a foreign currency, because of a shortage of hard currencies. This tends to be a short-term problem.
- *Transfer risk* is the inability to transfer funds across a national border, due to local-country regulatory restrictions on the movement of hard currencies out of the country. Thus, a company may find that a local subsidiary is extremely profitable, but the parent company cannot extract the profits from the country.

Country-specific risks call for strategic-level decisions in the executive suite, not in the treasury department. The senior management team must decide if it is willing to accept the risks of expropriation or of not being able to extract cash from a country. If not, the risk is eliminated by refusing to do business within the country.

Please note that the *type* of risk has a considerable impact on the time period over which a company is at risk. For example, transactional risk spans a relatively short period, from the signing date of the contract that initiates a sale, until the final payment date. The total interval may be only one or two months. However, translation risk and the various types of economic risks can extend over many years. There tends to be an inordinate focus in many companies on the short-term transactional risk, when more emphasis should be placed on hedging against these other risks that can result in substantial losses over the long term.

Foreign Exchange Risk Management

As noted in the last section, a company is at risk of incurring a loss due to fluctuations in any exchange rates that it must buy or sell as part of its business transactions. What can be done? Valid steps can range from no action at all to the active use of several types of hedges. In this section, we address the multitude of options available to mitigate foreign exchange-related risks. While perusing these options, keep in mind that the most sophisticated response is not necessarily the best response. In many cases, the circumstances may make it quite acceptable to take on some degree of risk, rather than engaging in a hedging strategy that is not only expensive, but also difficult to understand.

Take No Action

There are many situations where a company rarely engages in transactions that involve foreign exchange, and so does not want to spend time investigating how to reduce risk. There are other situations where the amounts of foreign exchange involved are so small that the risk level is immaterial. In either case, a company will be tempted to take no action, which may be a reasonable course of action, depending on the management team's tolerance for risk.

Avoid Risk

A company can avoid some types of risk by altering its strategy to completely sidestep the risk. Complete avoidance of a specific product, geographic region, or business line is an entirely reasonable alternative under the following circumstances:

- The potential loss from a risk condition is very high
- The probability of loss from a risk condition is very high
- It is difficult to develop a hedge against a risk
- The offsetting potential for profit does not offset the risk that will be incurred

For example, a company located in the United States buys the bulk of its supplies in China, and is required under its purchasing contracts to pay suppliers in yuan. If the company does not want to undertake the risk of exchange rate fluctuations in the yuan, it can consider altering its supply chain, so that it purchases within its home country, rather than in China. This alignment of sales and purchases within the same country to avoid foreign currency transactions is known as an *operational hedge*.

As another example, a company wants to sell products into a market where the government has just imposed severe restrictions on the cross-border transfer of funds out of the country. The government also has a history of nationalizing industries that had been privately-owned. Under these circumstances, it makes little sense for the company to sell into the new market if it cannot extract its profits, and if its assets in the country are subject to expropriation.

Shift Risk

When a company is either required to pay or receive payment in a foreign currency, it is taking on the risk associated with changes in the foreign currency exchange rate. This risk can be completely eliminated by requiring customers to pay in the company's home currency, or suppliers to accept payment in the company's home currency. This is a valid option when the company is a large one that can force this system of payment onto its suppliers, or when it sells a unique product that forces customers to accept the company's terms.

Tip: Never give customers a choice of currency in which to pay the company, since they will likely pay with their home currency, leaving the company to bear the risk of exchange rate changes.

Another possibility is to charge business partners for any changes in the exchange rate between the date of order placement and the shipment date. This is an extremely difficult business practice to enforce, for the following reasons:

- *Continual rebillings.* There will always be some degree of variation in exchange rates between the order date and shipment date, so it is probable that a company would have to issue an invoice related to exchange rate adjustments for every order, or at least include a line item for the change in every invoice.
- *Two-way rebillings.* If a company is going to insist on billing for its exchange rate losses, it is only fair that it pay back its business partners when exchange rates shift in its favor.
- *Purchase order limitations.* Customers routinely place orders using a purchase order than only authorizes a certain spending level. If the company later issues an incremental billing that exceeds the total amount authorized for a purchase, the customer will probably not pay the company.

To mitigate these issues, billing a business partner for a change in exchange rates should only be enacted if the change is sufficiently large to breach a contractually-agreed minimum level. The minimum level should be set so that this additional billing is a rare event.

EXAMPLE

An outsourcing company enters into long-term services contracts with its customers, and so is at considerable foreign exchange risk. It offers customers a fixed price contract within a 5% currency trading band, outside of which customers share the risk with the company. If the company gains from a currency shift outside of the trading band, it discounts the contract price.

The conditions under which currency risk can be shifted elsewhere are not common ones. Most companies will find that if they insist on only dealing in their home currencies, such behavior will either annoy suppliers or drive away customers. Thus, we will continue with other risk management actions that will be more palatable to a company's business partners.

Time Compression

Large variations in exchange rates are more likely to occur over longer periods of time than over shorter periods of time. Thus, it may be possible to reduce the risk of exchange rate fluctuations by reducing the contractually-mandated payment period. For example, 30 day payment terms could be compressed to 10 or 15 days. However, delays in shipping, customs inspections, and resistance from business partners can make it difficult to achieve a compressed payment schedule. Also, a customer being asked to accept a shorter payment schedule may attempt to push back with lower prices or other benefits, which increases the cost of this option.

The time compression concept can take the form of a company policy that does not allow standard credit terms to foreign customers that exceed a certain number of days. By doing so, a company can at least minimize the number of days during which exchange rates can fluctuate.

Payment Leading and Lagging

If there is a pronounced trend in exchange rates over the short term, the accounts payable manager can be encouraged to alter the timing normally associated with payables payments to take advantage of expected changes in exchange rates. For example, if a foreign currency is becoming more expensive, it may make sense to pay those payables denominated in it as soon as possible, rather than waiting until the normal payment date to pay in a more expensive currency. Similarly, if a foreign currency is declining in value, there may be an opportunity to delay payments by a few days to take advantage of the ongoing decline in the exchange rate. The latter case may be too much trouble, since suppliers do not appreciate late payments.

Build Reserves

If company management believes that there is just as great a risk of a gain as a loss on a currency fluctuation, it may be willing to accept the downside risk in hopes of attaining an upside profit. If so, it is possible to build cash and debt reserves greater than what would normally be needed, against the possibility of an outsized loss. This may entail investing a large amount of cash in very liquid investments, or retaining extra cash that might otherwise be paid out in dividends or used for capital expenditures. Other options are to obtain an unusually large line of credit that can be called upon in the event of a loss, or selling more stock than would typically be needed for operational purposes.

Building reserves will protect a business from foreign exchange risk, but the cost of acquiring and maintaining those reserves is substantial. Cash that is kept on hand could have earned an investment, while a commitment fee must be paid for a line of credit, even if the line is never used. Similarly, investors who buy a company's stock expect to earn a return. Thus, there is a noticeable cost associated with building reserves. A less-expensive option is hedging, which we will address shortly.

Maintain Local Reserves

If the company is routinely engaging in the purchase and sale of goods and services within another country, the answer may be to maintain a cash reserve within that country, which is denominated in the local currency. Doing so eliminates the cost of repeatedly buying and selling currencies and paying the related conversion commissions. The downside of maintaining local reserves is that a company is still subject to translation risk, where it must periodically translate its local cash reserves into its home currency for financial reporting purposes – which carries with it the risk of recording a translation loss.

Hedging

When all operational and strategic alternatives have been exhausted, it is time to consider buying hedging instruments that offset the risk posed by specific foreign exchange positions. Hedging is accomplished by purchasing an offsetting currency exposure. For example, if a company has a liability to deliver 1 million euros in six months, it can hedge this risk by entering into a contract to purchase 1 million euros on the same date, so that it can buy and sell in the same currency on the same date. The ideal outcome of a hedge is when the distribution of probable outcomes is reduced, so that the size of any potential loss is reduced. The following exhibit shows the effect of hedging on the range of possible outcomes.

Impact of Hedging on Risk Outcome

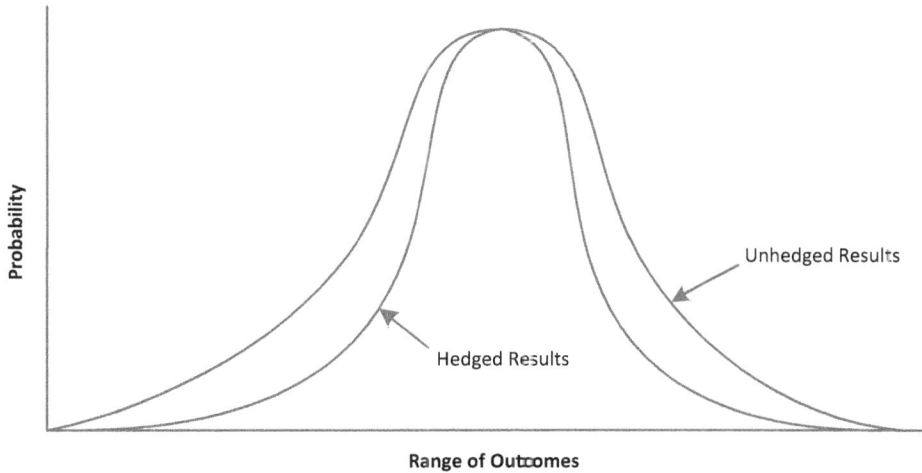

Probability (y-axis)

Unhedged Results

Hedged Results

Range of Outcomes (x-axis)

When a company has a multi-year contract with a customer, it may be necessary to create a long-term hedge to offset the related risk of currency fluctuations. If the customer subsequently terminates the contract early, the company may have to incur a significant cost to unwind the related hedge before its planned termination date. If this scenario appears possible, or if a business has experienced such events in the past, it may make sense to include in the contract a clause stating that the customer bears the cost of unwinding the hedge if there is an early contract termination.

Tip: When entering into a long-term contract for which a hedge is anticipated, be sure to estimate the cost of the hedge in advance, and include it in the formulation of the price quoted to the customer.

Summary

Clearly, there are many risk management alternatives available to a company that must deal with foreign exchange situations. We recommend avoiding active hedging strategies as long as possible, in favor of more passive methods that are easier to understand, implement, and monitor. If the risk situation is too extreme to be completely addressed by passive means, then an active hedging strategy is probably the answer. In the next section, we address several types of active hedging transactions.

Types of Foreign Exchange Hedges

This section describes a number of methods for hedging foreign currency transactions. The first type of hedge, which is a loan denominated in a foreign currency, is designed to offset translation risk. The remaining hedges target the transaction risk related to the currency fluctuations associated with either specific or aggregated business transactions.

Loan Denominated in a Foreign Currency

When a company is at risk of recording a loss from the translation of assets and liabilities into its home currency, it can hedge the risk by obtaining a loan denominated in the functional currency in which the assets and liabilities are recorded. The effect of this hedge is to neutralize any loss on translation of the subsidiary's net assets with a gain on translation of the loan, or vice versa.

EXAMPLE

Hammer Industries has a subsidiary located in London, and which does business entirely within England. Accordingly, the subsidiary's net assets are denominated in pounds. The net assets of the subsidiary are currently recorded at £10 million. To hedge the translation risk associated with these assets, Hammer acquires a £10 million loan from a bank in London.

One month later, a change in the dollar/pound exchange rate results in a translation loss of $15,000 on the translation of the subsidiary's net assets into U.S. dollars. This amount is exactly offset by the translation gain of $15,000 on the liability associated with the £10 million loan.

Tip: An ideal way to create an offsetting loan is to fund the purchase or expansion of a foreign subsidiary largely through the proceeds of a long-term loan obtained within the same country, so that the subsidiary's assets are approximately cancelled out by the amount of the loan.

There are two problems with this type of hedge. First, it can be difficult to obtain a loan in the country in which the net assets are located. Second, the company will incur an interest expense on a loan that it would otherwise not need, though the borrowed funds could be invested to offset the interest expense.

The Forward Contract

A forward contract is an agreement under which a business agrees to buy a certain amount of foreign currency on a specific future date, and at a predetermined exchange rate. Forward exchange rates can be obtained for twelve months into the future; quotes for major currency pairs can be obtained for as much as five to ten years in the future. The exchange rate is comprised of the following elements:

- The spot price of the currency
- The bank's transaction fee
- An adjustment (up or down) for the interest rate differential between the two currencies. In essence, the currency of the country having a lower interest rate will trade at a premium, while the currency of the country having a higher interest rate will trade at a discount. For example, if the domestic interest rate is lower than the rate in the other country, the bank acting as the counterparty

adds points to the spot rate, which increases the cost of the foreign currency in the forward contract.

The calculation of the number of discount or premium points to subtract from or add to a forward contract is based on the following formula:

$$\text{Exchange rate} \quad \times \quad \text{Interest rate differential} \quad \times \quad \frac{\text{Days in contract}}{360} \quad = \quad \text{Premium or discount}$$

Thus, if the spot price of pounds per dollar were 1.5459 and there were a premium of 15 points for a forward contract with a 360-day maturity, the forward rate (not including a transaction fee) would be 1.5474.

By entering into a forward contract, a company can ensure that a definite future liability can be settled at a specific exchange rate. Forward contracts are typically customized, and arranged between a company and its bank. The bank will require a partial payment to initiate a forward contract, as well as final payment shortly before the settlement date.

EXAMPLE

Hammer Industries has acquired equipment from a company in the United Kingdom, which Hammer must pay for in 60 days in the amount of £150,000. To hedge against the risk of an unfavorable change in exchange rates during the intervening 60 days, Hammer enters into a forward contract with its bank to buy £150,000 in 60 days, at the current exchange rate.

60 days later, the exchange rate has indeed taken a turn for the worse, but Hammer's treasurer is indifferent, since he obtains the £150,000 needed for the purchase transaction based on the exchange rate in existence when the contract with the supplier was originally signed.

A forward contract is designed to have a specific settlement date, but the business transaction to which it relates may not be so timely. For example, a business has a contract to sell £10,000 in 60 days, but may not be able to do so if it has not yet received funds from a customer. A *forward window contract* is designed to work around this variability in the timing of receipts from customers by incorporating a range of settlement dates. One can then wait for a cash receipt and trigger settlement of the forward contract immediately thereafter.

The primary difficulties with forward contracts relate to their being customized transactions that are designed specifically for two parties. Because of this level of customization, it is difficult for either party to offload the contract to a third party. Also, the level of customization makes it difficult to compare offerings from different banks, so there is a tendency for banks to build unusually large fees into these contracts. Finally, a company may find that the underlying transaction for which a forward contract was created has been cancelled, leaving the contract still to be settled. If so, one can enter into a second forward contract, whose net effect is to offset the first forward contract. Though the bank will charge fees for both contracts, this arrangement will settle the company's obligations.

The Futures Contract

A futures contract is similar in concept to a forward contract, in that a business can enter into a contract to buy or sell currency at a specific price on a future date. The difference is that futures contracts are traded on an exchange, so these contracts are for standard amounts and durations. An initial deposit into a margin account is required to initiate a futures contract. The contract is then repriced each day, and if cumulative losses drain the margin account, a company is required to add more funds to the margin account. If the company does not respond to a margin call, the exchange closes out the contract.

Given that futures contracts are standardized, they may not exactly match the timing and amounts of an underlying transaction that is being hedged, which can lead to over- or under-hedging. However, since these contracts are traded on an exchange, it is easier to trade them than forward contracts, which allows for the easy unwinding of a hedge position earlier than its normal settlement date.

In a forward contract, the bank includes a transaction fee in the contract. In a futures contract, a broker charges a commission to execute the deal.

The Currency Option

An option gives its owner the right, but not the obligation, to buy or sell an asset at a certain price (known as the *strike price*), either on or before a specific date. In exchange for this right, the buyer pays an up-front premium to the seller. The income earned by the seller is restricted to the premium payment received, while the buyer has a theoretically unlimited profit potential, depending upon the future direction of the relevant exchange rate.

Currency options are available for the purchase or sale of currencies within a certain future date range, with the following variations available for the option contract:

- *American option.* The option can be exercised on any date within the option period, so that delivery is two business days after the exercise date.
- *European option.* The option can only be exercised on the expiry date, which means that delivery will be two business days after the expiry date.
- *Burmudan option.* The option can only be exercised on certain predetermined dates.

The holder of an option will exercise it when the strike price is more favorable than the current market rate, which is called being *in-the-money*. If the strike price is less favorable than the current market rate, this is called being *out-of-the-money*, in which case the option holder will not exercise the option. If the option holder is inattentive, it is possible that an in-the-money option will not be exercised prior to its expiry date. Notice of option exercise must be given to the counterparty by the notification date stated in the option contract.

A currency option provides two key benefits:

- *Loss prevention*. An option can be exercised to hedge the risk of loss, while still leaving open the possibility of benefiting from a favorable change in exchange rates.
- *Date variability*. The holder can exercise an option within a predetermined date range, which is useful when there is uncertainty about the exact timing of the underlying exposure.

There are a number of factors that enter into the price of a currency option, which can make it difficult to ascertain whether a quoted option price is reasonable. These factors are:

- The difference between the designated strike price and the current spot price. The buyer of an option can choose a strike price that suits his specific circumstances. A strike price that is well away from the current spot price will cost less, since the likelihood of exercising the option is low. However, setting such a strike price means that the buyer is willing to absorb the loss associated with a significant change in the exchange rate before seeking cover behind an option.
- The current interest rates for the two currencies during the option period.
- The duration of the option.
- The volatility of the market. This is the expected amount by which the currency is expected to fluctuate during the option period, with higher volatility making it more likely that an option will be exercised. Volatility is a guesstimate, since there is no quantifiable way to predict it.
- The willingness of counterparties to issue options.

Banks generally allow an option exercise period of no more than three months. Multiple partial currency deliveries within a currency option can be arranged.

Exchange traded options for standard quantities are available. This type of option eliminates the risk of counterparty failure, since the clearing house operating the exchange guarantees the performance of all options traded on the exchange.

EXAMPLE

Hammer Industries has an obligation to buy £250,000 in three months. Currently, the forward rate for the British pound is 1.5000 U.S. dollars, so that it should require $375,000 to buy the £250,000 in 90 days. If the pound depreciates, Hammer will be able to buy pounds for less than the $375,000 that it currently anticipates spending, but if the pound appreciates, Hammer will have to spend more to acquire the £250,000.

Hammer's treasurer elects to buy an option, so that he can hedge against the appreciation of the pound, while leaving open the prospect of profits to be gained from any depreciation in the pound. The cost of an option with a strike price of 1.6000 U.S. dollars per pound is $3,000.

Three months later, the pound has appreciated against the dollar, with the price having changed to 1.75 U.S. dollars per pound. The treasurer exercises the option, and spends $400,000 for the requisite number of pounds (calculated as £250,000 × 1.6000). If he had not purchased the option, the purchase would instead have cost $437,500 (calculated as £250,000 × 1.7500). Thus, Hammer saved $34,500 by using a currency option (calculated as the savings of $37,500, less the $3,000 cost of the option).

Currency options are particularly valuable during periods of high currency price volatility. Unfortunately from the perspective of the buyer, high volatility equates to higher option prices, since there is a higher probability that the counterparty will have to make a payment to the option buyer.

The Cylinder Option

Two options can be combined to create a *cylinder option*. One option is priced above the current spot price of the target currency, while the other option is priced below the spot price. The gain from exercising one option is used to partially offset the cost of the other option, thereby reducing the overall cost of the hedge. In effect, the upside potential offered by one option is being sold for a premium payment in order to finance the protection afforded by the opposing option.

The cylinder option is configured so that a company can acquire the right to buy currency at a specified price (a call option) and sell an option to a counterparty to buy currency from the company at a specified price (a put option), usually as of the expiry date. The premium the company pays for the purchased call is partially offset by the premium payable to the company for the put option that it sold.

If the market exchange rate remains between the boundaries established by the two currency options, the company never uses its options and instead buys or sells currency on the open market to fulfill its currency needs. If the market price breaches the strike price of the call option, the company exercises the call option and buys currency at the designated strike price. Conversely, if the market price breaches the strike price of the put option, the counterparty exercises its option to sell the currency to the company.

A variation on the cylinder option is to construct call and put options that are very close together, so that the premium cost of the call is very close to the premium income generated by the put, resulting in a near-zero net hedging cost to the company. The two options have to be very close together for the zero cost option to work, which means that the effective currency price range being hedged is quite small.

Swaps

If a company has or expects to have an obligation to make a payment in a foreign currency, it can arrange to swap currency holdings with a third party that already has the required currency. The two entities engage in a swap transaction by agreeing upon an initial swap date, the date when the cash positions will be reversed back to their original positions, and an interest rate that reflects the comparative differences in interest rates between the two countries in which the entities are located.

Another use for a currency swap is when a forward exchange contract has been delayed. In this situation, one would normally sell to a counterparty the currency that it has just obtained through the receipt of an account receivable. If, however, the receivable has not yet been paid, the company can enter into a swap agreement to obtain the required currency and meet its immediate obligation under the forward exchange contract. Later, when the receivable is eventually paid, the company can reverse the swap, returning funds to the counterparty.

A swap arrangement may be for just a one-day period, or extend out for several years into the future. Swap transactions generally do not occur in amounts of less than $5 million, so this technique is not available to smaller businesses.

A potentially serious problem with swaps is the prospect of a default by the counterparty. If there is a default, the company once again assumes its foreign currency liability, and must now scramble to find an alternative hedge.

Netting

There are circumstances where a company has subsidiaries in multiple countries that actively trade with each other. If so, they should have accounts receivable and payable with each other, which could give rise to a flurry of foreign exchange transactions in multiple currencies that could trigger any number of hedging activities. It may be possible to reduce the amount of hedging activity through *payment netting*, where the corporate parent offsets all accounts receivable and payable against each other to determine the net amount of foreign exchange transactions that actually require hedges. A centralized netting function may be used, which means that each subsidiary either receives a single payment from the netting center, or makes a single payment to the netting center. Netting results in the following benefits:

- Foreign exchange exposure is no longer tracked at the subsidiary level
- The total amount of foreign exchange purchased and sold declines, which reduces the amount of foreign exchange commissions paid out
- The total amount of cash in transit (and therefore not available for investment) between subsidiaries declines

Tip: It is easier to create an intracompany netting system when there is already a centralized accounts payable function for the entire business, which is called a *payment factory*.

Intracompany netting will still result in some payments between subsidiaries located in different countries. Since each subsidiary may be operating its own cash concentration system, this means that cash must be physically shifted from one cash pool to another, which is inefficient. Where possible, consider creating cash pools that span international boundaries, so that there is no need for cross-border transfers between cash pools. The result is essentially free cash transfers within the company.

The same concept can be applied to payables and receivables with outside entities, though a considerable amount of information sharing is needed to make the concept work. In some industries where there is a high level of trade between companies, industry-wide netting programs have been established that routinely offset a large proportion of the payables and receivables within the industry. The net result is that all offsetting obligations are reduced to a single payment per currency per value date between counterparties.

A related concept is *close-out netting*, where counterparties having forward contracts with each other can agree to net the obligations, rather than engaging in a large number of individual contract settlements. Before engaging in close-out netting, discuss the concept with corporate counsel. A case has been made in some jurisdictions that close-out netting runs counter to the interests of other creditors in the event of a bankruptcy by one of the counterparties.

The only downside of netting is that the accounting departments of the participating companies must sort out how their various transactions are settled. This requires a procedure for splitting a group of netted transactions into individual payments and receipts in the cash receipts and accounts payable modules of their accounting systems.

Interest Risk Overview

Interest rate risk involves the risk of increases in interest rates on debt, as well as reductions in interest rates for investment instruments, with the attendant negative impact on profitability. This risk can take the following forms:

- *Absolute rate changes*. The market rate of interest will move up or down over time, resulting in immediate variances from the interest rates paid or earned by a company. This rate change is easily monitored.
- *Reinvestment risk*. Investments must be periodically re-invested and debt reissued. If interest rates happen to be unfavorable during one of these rollover periods, a company will be forced to accept whatever interest rate is available.
- *Yield curve risk*. The yield curve shows the relationship between short-term and long-term interest rates, and typically slopes upward to indicate that long-term debt carries a higher interest rate to reflect the risk to the lender associated with such debt. If the yield curve steepens, flattens, or declines, these relationships change the debt duration that a company should use in its borrowing and investing strategies.

Interest risk is a particular concern for those businesses using large amounts of debt to fund their operations, since even a small increase in the interest rate could have a profound impact on profits, when multiplied by the volume of debt employed. Further, a sudden boost in interest expense could worsen a company's interest coverage ratio, which is a common covenant in loan agreements, and which could trigger a loan termination if the minimum ratio covenant is not met.

Interest Rate Risk Management

The primary objective of interest risk management is to keep fluctuations in interest rates from impacting company earnings. Management can respond to this objective in many ways, ranging from a conscious decision to take no action, passing through a number of relatively passive alternatives, and culminating in several active techniques for risk mitigation. We provide an overview of each option in this section.

Take No Action

There may be situations where a company has minimal investments that earn interest, or issues only minor amounts of debt. If so, it is certainly acceptable to not implement an aggressive risk management campaign related to interest rates. However, this state of affairs does not typically last for long, after which there will be some degree of risk related to interest rates. In anticipation of such an event, it is useful to model the amount of interest rate change that must occur before there will be a serious impact on company finances. Once that trigger point is known, the treasurer can begin to prepare any of the risk mitigation alternatives noted later in this section.

Avoid Risk

The risk associated with interest rates arises between external entities and a business; it does not arise between the subsidiaries of the same business. Thus, a company can act as its own bank to some extent, by providing intercompany lending arrangements at interest rates that are not subject to fluctuations. This is particularly useful in a multi-national corporation, where cash reserves in different currencies may be scattered throughout the business, and can be lent back and forth to cover immediate cash needs.

Another way to avoid risk is to operate the business in such a conservative manner that the company has no debt, thereby eliminating the risk associated with interest rates on debt. The same result can be achieved by using invested funds to pay off any outstanding debt. The main downside of the low-debt method is that a company may be constraining its growth by not taking advantage of a low-cost source of funds (i.e., debt).

Asset and Liability Matching

A key trigger for interest rate risk is when short-term debt is used to fund an asset that is expected to be held for a long period of time. In this situation, the short-term debt must be rolled over multiple times during the life span of the asset or until the debt is paid off, introducing the risk that each successive debt rollover will result in an increased interest rate. To avoid this risk, arrange for financing that approximately matches the useful life of the underlying asset. Thus, spending $1 million for a machine that is expected to have a useful life of 10 years should be funded with a loan that also has a 10-year life.

Hedging

Interest rate hedging is the practice of acquiring financial instruments whose effects offset those of the underlying scenario causing interest rate fluctuations, so that the net effect is minimized rate fluctuations. Hedges fall into two categories:

- *Forward rate agreements and futures*. These financial instruments are designed to lock in an interest rate, so that changes in the actual interest rate above or below the baseline interest rate do not impact a business. These instruments do not provide any flexibility for taking advantage of favorable changes in interest rates.
- *Options*. These financial instruments only lock in an interest rate if the holder wants to do so, thereby presenting the possibility of benefiting from a favorable change in an interest rate.

The various types of interest rate hedges are discussed next.

Types of Interest Rate Hedges

This section describes a number of methods for hedging the variability in interest rates. These options are mostly designed for high-value transactions, and so are not available to smaller companies.

The Forward Rate Agreement

A forward rate agreement (FRA) is an agreement between two parties to lock in a specific interest rate for a designated period of time, which usually spans just a few months. Under an FRA, the parties are protecting against opposing exposures: the FRA buyer wants to protect against an increase in the interest rate, while the FRA seller wants to protect against a decrease in the interest rate. Any payout under an FRA is based on a change in the reference interest rate from the interest rate stated in the contract (the FRA rate). An FRA is not related to a specific loan or investment – it simply provides interest rate protection.

The FRA rate is based on the yield curve, where interest rates usually increase for instruments having longer maturities. This means that the FRA rate typically increases for periods further in the future.

Several date-specific terms are referred to in a forward rate agreement, and are crucial to understanding how the FRA concept works. These terms are:

1. *Contract date*. The date on which the FRA begins.
2. *Expiry date*. The date on which any variance between the market rate and the reference rate is calculated.
3. *Settlement date*. The date on which the interest variance is paid by one counterparty to the other.
4. *Maturity date*. The final date of the date range that underlies the FRA contract.

In essence, these four dates anchor the two time periods covered by an FRA. The first period, which begins with the contract date and ends with the expiry date, spans the term of the contract. The second period begins with the settlement date and ends with the maturity date, and spans the period that underlies the contract. This date range is shown graphically in the following example.

Relevant FRA Dates

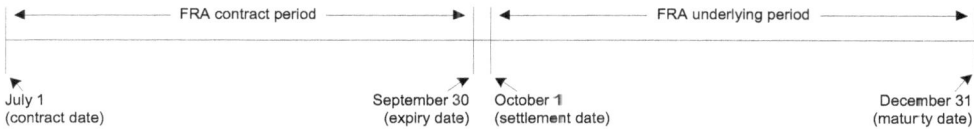

| ◄─────── FRA contract period ───────► | ◄─────── FRA underlying period ───────► |
| July 1 (contract date) | September 30 (expiry date) | October 1 (settlement date) | December 31 (maturity date) |

The FRA rate is based on a future period, such as the period starting in one month and ending in four months, which is said to have a "1×4" FRA term, and has an effective term of three months. Similarly, a contract starting in three months and ending in six months is said to have a "3×6" FRA term, and also has an effective term of three months.

At the *beginning* of the designated FRA period, the interest rate stated in the contract is compared to the reference rate. The reference rate is usually a well-known interest rate index, such as the London Interbank Offered Rate (LIBOR). If the reference rate is higher, the seller makes a payment to the FRA buyer, based on the incremental difference in interest rates and the notional amount of the contract. The payment calculation is shown in the following example. If the reference rate is lower than the interest rate stated in the contract, the buyer makes a payment to the FRA seller. The payment made between the counterparties must be discounted to its present value, since the payment is associated with the FRA underlying period that has not yet happened. Thus, the discount assumes that the money would actually be due on the maturity date, but is payable on the settlement date (which may be months before the maturity date). The calculation for discounting the payment between counterparties is:

$$\frac{\text{Settlement amount}}{1 + (\text{Days in FRA underlying period}/360 \text{ Days} \times \text{Reference rate})} = \frac{\text{Discounted}}{\text{Payment}}$$

The reason why the contract payment is calculated at the *beginning* of the designated FRA period is that the risk being hedged by the contract was from the initial contract date until the date on which the FRA buyer expects to borrow money and lock in an interest rate. For example, a company may enter into an FRA in January, because it is uncertain of what the market interest rate will be in April, when it intends to borrow funds; the period at risk is therefore from January through April. The following example illustrates the concept.

EXAMPLE

Hammer Industries has a legal commitment to borrow $50 million in two months, and for a period of three months. Hammer's treasurer is concerned that there may be an increase in the interest rate during the two-month period prior to borrowing the $50 million. The treasurer elects to hedge the risk of an increase in the interest rate by purchasing a three-month FRA, starting in two months. A broker quotes a rate of 5.50%. Hammer enters into an FRA at the 5.50% interest rate, with 3rd National Bank as the counterparty. The notional amount of the contract is for $50 million.

Two months later, the reference rate is 6.00%, so 3rd National pays Hammer the difference between the contract rate and reference rate, which is 0.50%. At the same time, Hammer borrows $50 million at the market rate (which happens to match the reference rate) of 6.00%. Because of the FRA, Hammer's effective borrowing rate is 5.50%.

The amount paid by 3rd National to Hammer is calculated as:

(Reference rate − FRA rate) × (FRA days/360 days) × Notional amount = Profit or loss

or

(6.00% - 5.50%) × (90 days/360 days) × $50 million = $62,500

Since the payment is made at the beginning of the borrowing period, rather than at its end, the $62,500 payment is discounted and its present value paid. The discounting calculation for the settlement amount is:

$$\frac{\$62,500}{1 + (90/360 \text{ Days} \times 6.00\%)} = \$61,576.35$$

What if the reference rate had fallen by 0.50%, instead of increasing? Then Hammer would have paid 3rd National the discounted amount of $62,500, rather than the reverse. Hammer would also end up borrowing the $50 million at the new market rate of 5.00%. When the payment to 3rd National is combined with the reduced 5.00% interest rate, Hammer will still be paying a 5.50% interest rate, which is what it wanted all along.

From the buyer's perspective, the result of an FRA is that it pays the expected interest rate – no higher, and no lower.

The Futures Contract

An interest rate futures contract is conceptually similar to a forward contract, except that it is traded on an exchange, which means that it is for a standard amount and duration. The standard size of a futures contract is $1 million, so multiple contracts may need to be purchased to create a hedge for a specific loan or investment amount. The pricing for futures contracts starts at a baseline figure of 100, and declines based on the implied interest rate in a contract. For example, if a futures contract has an implied interest rate of 5.00%, the price of that contract will be 95.00. The calculation of the profit or loss on a futures contract is derived as follows:

Notional contract amount × Contract duration/360 Days × (Ending price – Beginning price)

Most trading in interest rate futures is in Eurodollars (U.S. dollars held outside of the United States), and are traded on the Chicago Mercantile Exchange.

Hedging is not perfect, since the notional amount of a contract may vary from the actual amount of funding that a company wants to hedge, resulting in a modest amount of either over- or under-hedging. For example, hedging a $15.4 million position will require the purchase of either 15 or 16 $1 million contracts. There may also be differences between the time period required for a hedge and the actual hedge period as stated in a futures contract. For example, if there is a seven month exposure to be hedged, a treasurer could acquire two consecutive three-month contracts, and elect to have the seventh month be unhedged.

> **Tip:** If the buyer wants to protect against interest rate variability for a longer period, such as for the next year, it is possible to buy a series of futures contracts covering consecutive periods, so that coverage is achieved for the entire time period.

EXAMPLE

The treasurer of Hammer Industries wants to hedge an investment of $10 million. To do so, he sells 10 three-month futures contracts with contract terms of three months. The current three-month LIBOR is 3.50% and the 3 × 6 forward rate is 3.75%. These contracts are currently listed on the Chicago Mercantile Exchange at 96.25, which is calculated as 100 minus the 3.75% forward rate.

When the futures contracts expire, the forward rate has declined to 3.65%, so that the contracts are now listed at 96.35 (calculated as 100 – the 3.65 percent forward rate). By engaging in this hedge, Hammer has earned a profit of $2,500, which is calculated as follows:

$$\$10,000,000 \times (90/360) \times (0.9635 \text{ Ending price} - 0.9625 \text{ Beginning price})$$

$$= \$2,500$$

When the buyer purchases a futures contract, a minimum amount must initially be posted in a margin account to ensure performance under the contract terms. It may be necessary to fund the margin account with additional cash (a *margin call*) if the market value of the contract declines over time (margin accounts are revised daily, based on the market closing price). If the buyer cannot provide additional funding in the event of a contract decline, the futures exchange closes out the contract prior to its normal termination date. Conversely, if the market value of the contract increases, the net gain is credited to the buyer's margin account. On the last day of the contract, the exchange marks the contract to market and settles the accounts of the buyer and seller. Thus, transfers between buyers and sellers over the life of a contract are essentially a zero-sum game, where one party directly benefits at the expense of the other.

It is also possible to enter into a bond futures contract, which can be used to hedge interest rate risk. For example, a business that has borrowed funds can hedge against rising interest rates by selling a bond futures contract. Then, if interest rates do in fact rise, the resulting gain on the contract will offset the higher interest rate that the borrower is paying. Conversely, if interest rates subsequently fall, the borrower will experience a loss on the contract, which will offset the lower interest rate now being paid. Thus, the net effect of the contract is that the borrower locks in the beginning interest rate through the period of the contract.

> **Tip:** A bond futures contract is not a perfect hedge, for it is also impacted by changes in the credit rating of the bond issuer.

When a purchased futures contract expires, it is customary to settle it by selling a futures contract that has the same delivery date. Conversely, if the original contract was sold to a counterparty, then the seller can settle the contract by buying a futures contract that has the same delivery date.

The following table notes the key differences between forward rate agreements and futures contracts. Similarities between the two instruments are excluded from the table.

Differences between a Futures Contract and FRA

Feature	Futures Contract	Forward Rate Agreement
Trading platform	Exchange-based	Between two parties
Counterparty	The exchange	Single counterparty
Collateral	Margin account	None
Agreement	Standardized	Modified
Settlement	Daily mark to market	On expiry date

The preceding table reveals two key differences between a futures contract and an FRA. First, there can be significant counterparty risk in an FRA, since the contract period can be lengthy, and financial conditions can change markedly over that time. Second, a futures contract is settled every day, which can create pressure to fund a margin call if there are significant losses on the contract.

The Interest Rate Swap

An interest rate swap is a customized contract between two parties to swap two schedules of cash flows that could extend for anywhere from one to 25 years, and which represent interest payments. Only the interest rate obligations are swapped, not the underlying loans or investments from which the obligations are derived. The counterparties are usually a company and a bank. There are many types of rate swaps; we will confine this discussion to a swap arrangement where one schedule of cash flows is based on a floating interest rate, and the other is based on a fixed interest rate. For example, a five-year schedule of cash flows based on a fixed interest rate may be swapped for a five-year schedule of cash flows based on a floating interest rate that is tied to the London Interbank Offered Rate (LIBOR).

The most common reason to engage in an interest rate swap is to exchange a variable-rate payment for a fixed-rate payment, or vice versa. Thus, a company that has only been able to obtain a floating-rate loan can effectively convert the loan to a fixed-rate loan through an interest rate swap. This approach is especially attractive when a borrower is only able to obtain a fixed-rate loan by paying a premium, but can combine a variable-rate loan and an interest rate swap to achieve a fixed-rate loan at a lower price.

A company may want to take the reverse approach and swap its fixed interest payments for floating payments. This situation arises when the treasurer believes that interest rates will decline during the swap period, and wants to take advantage of the lower rates.

A swap contract is settled through a multi-step process, which is:

1. Calculate the payment obligation of each party, typically once every six months through the life of the swap arrangement.
2. Determine the variance between the two amounts.
3. The party whose position is improved by the swap arrangement pays the variance to the party whose position is degraded by the swap arrangement.

Thus, a company continues to pay interest to its banker under the original lending agreement, while the company either accepts a payment from the rate swap counterparty, or issues a payment to the counterparty, with the result being that the net amount of interest paid by the company is the amount planned by the business when it entered into the swap agreement.

EXAMPLE

Hammer Industries has a $15 million variable-rate loan outstanding that matures in two years. The current interest rate on the loan is 6.5%. Hammer enters into an interest rate swap agreement with Big Regional Bank for a fixed-rate 7.0% loan with a $15 million notional amount. The first scheduled payment swap date is in six months. On that date, the variable rate on Hammer's loan has increased to 7.25%. Thus, the total interest payments on the swap date are $543,750 for Hammer and $525,000 for Big Regional. Since the two parties have agreed to swap payments, Big Regional pays Hammer the difference between the two payments, which is $18,750.

Hammer issues an interest payment of $543,750 to its bank. When netted with the cash inflow of $18,750 from Big Regional, this means that the net interest rate being paid by Hammer is 7.0%.

Several larger banks have active trading groups that routinely deal with interest rate swaps. Most swaps involve sums in the millions of dollars, but some banks are willing to engage in swap arrangements involving amounts of less than $1 million. There is a counterparty risk with interest rate swaps, since one party could fail to make a contractually-mandated payment to the other party. This risk is of particular concern when a swap arrangement covers multiple years, since the financial condition of a counterparty could change dramatically during that time.

If there is general agreement in the marketplace that interest rates are headed in a certain direction, it will be more expensive to obtain a swap that protects against interest rate changes in the anticipated direction.

Interest Rate Options

An option gives its owner the right, but not the obligation, to trigger a contract. The contract can be either a call option or a put option. A *call option* related to interest rates protects the option owner from rising interest rates, while a *put option* protects the option owner from declining interest rates. The party selling an option does so in exchange for a one-time premium payment. The party buying an option is doing so to mitigate its risk related to a change in interest rates.

An interest rate option can be relatively inexpensive if there has been or is expected to be little volatility in interest rates, since the option seller does not expect interest rates to move enough for the option to be exercised. Conversely, if there has been or is expected to be significant interest rate volatility, the option seller must assume that the option will be exercised, and so sets a higher price. Thus, periods of high interest rate volatility may make it cost-prohibitive to buy options.

> **Tip:** An interest rate hedge using an option may not be entirely successful if the reference rate used for the option is not the same one used for the underlying loan. For example, the reference rate for an option may be LIBOR, while the rate used for the underlying loan may be a bank's prime rate. The result is a hedging mismatch that can create an unplanned gain or loss.

An interest rate option sets a *strike price*, which is a specific interest rate at which the option buyer can borrow or lend money. The contract also states the amount of funds that the option buyer can borrow or lend (the *notional amount*). Rate increases and declines are measured using a *reference rate*, which is typically a well-known interest rate index, such as LIBOR. There is also an option expiration date, or *expiry date*, after which the option is cancelled. The buyer can specify the exact terms needed to hedge an interest rate position with a customized option.

If an option buyer wants to be protected from increases in interest rates, a *cap* (or ceiling) is created. A cap is a consecutive series of options, all having the same strike price. The buyer of a cap is paid whenever the reference rate exceeds the cap strike price on an option expiry date. For example, if a company wants to hedge its interest risk for one year with a strike price of 6.50%, beginning on January 1, it can buy the options noted in the following table.

Interest Rate Hedging Options

Desired Coverage Period	Option Number	Expiry Date	Option Term	Strike Price
January - March	--	Not applicable*	Not available*	N/A*
April - June	1	April 1	4 to 6 months	6.50%
July – September	2	July 1	7 to 9 months	6.50%
October - December	3	October 1	10 to 12 months	6.50%

* There is no option available for the first three-month period, since the expiry date is at the beginning of the contract period, so the expiry date will be reached immediately.

With a cap arrangement, the buyer is only subject to interest rate changes up to the cap, and is protected from rate changes above the cap if the reference rate exceeds the cap strike price on predetermined dates. If the reference interest rate is below the cap at the option expiration, the option buyer lets the option expire. However, if the reference rate is above the cap, the buyer exercises the option, which means that the option seller must reimburse the buyer for the difference between the reference rate and the cap rate, multiplied by the notional amount of the contract.

A cap may be included in a loan agreement, such that the borrower is guaranteed not to pay more than a designated maximum interest rate over the term of the loan, or for a predetermined portion of the loan. In this case, the lender has paid for the cap, and will probably include its cost in the interest rate or fees associated with the loan.

If a treasurer wants to be protected from decreases in interest rates (for invested funds), a *floor* is structured into an option, so that the option buyer is paid if the reference rate declines below the floor strike rate.

EXAMPLE

Hammer Industries has a $25 million 3-month loan that currently carries a fixed interest rate of 7.00%. Hammer's bank refuses to grant a fixed-rate loan for a longer time period, so Hammer plans to continually roll over the loan every three months. Recently, short-term interest rates have been spiking, so the treasurer decided to purchase an interest rate cap that is set at 7.50%, and which is comprised of two consecutive options, each with a three-month term.

At the expiry date of the first option, the reference rate is 7.25%, which is below the cap strike rate. The treasurer lets the option expire unused and rolls over the short-term loan at the new 7.25% rate.

At the next option expiry date, the reference rate has risen to 7.75%, which is 0.25% above the cap strike rate. The treasurer exercises the option, which forces the counterparty to pay Hammer for the difference between the cap strike rate and the reference rate. The calculation of the amount to be reimbursed is:

(Reference rate – Strike rate) × (Lending period/360 days) × Notional amount = Profit or loss

or

(7.75% - 7.50%) × (90/360) × $25 million = $15,625

Of course, the cost of the option reduces the benefits gained from an interest rate option, but still is useful for providing protection from outsized changes in interest rates.

> **Tip:** From an analysis perspective, it is useful to include the premium on an option with the amount of interest paid on a loan and any proceeds or payments associated with an exercised option, in order to derive the aggregate interest rate on any associated debt being hedged.

The cylinder option described earlier for foreign exchange risk can also be applied to interest rates. Under this concept, a company purchases a cap and sells a floor, with the current reference rate located between the two strike rates. The gain from exercising one option is used to partially offset the cost of the other option, which reduces the overall cost of the hedge. The three possible outcomes to this *collar* arrangement are:

1. The reference rate remains between the cap and floor, so neither option is exercised.
2. The reference rate rises above the cap, so the company is paid for the difference between the reference rate and the cap strike rate, multiplied by the notional amount of the contract.
3. The reference rate falls below the floor, so the company pays the option counterparty for the difference between the reference rate and the floor strike rate, multiplied by the notional amount of the contract.

The functioning of a collar arrangement is shown in the following exhibit, where the cap is set at 5% and the floor is set at 3%. No option is triggered until the reference rate drops to 2% in one of the later quarters, and again when it rises to 6%. In the first case, the company pays the 1% difference between the 3% floor and the 2% reference rate. In the latter case, the company is paid the 1% difference between the 5% cap and the 6% reference rate.

The Operation of an Interest Rate Collar

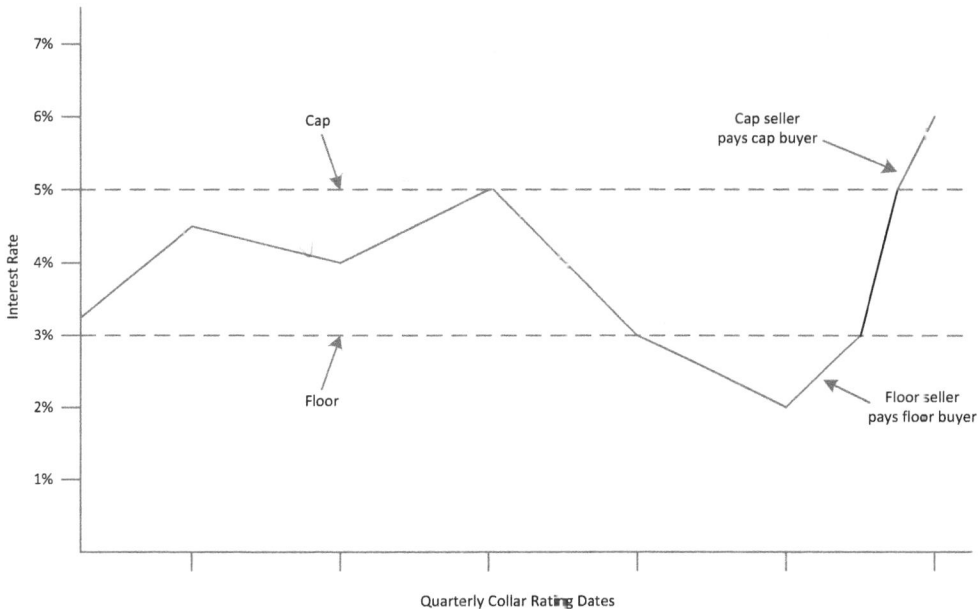

From the perspective of a company using a collar arrangement, the net effect is that interest rates will fluctuate only within the bounds set by the cap and floor strike rates.

A variation on the interest rate option concept is to include a call feature in a debt issuance. A call feature allows a company to buy back its debt from debt holders. The feature is quite useful in cases where the market interest rate has fallen since debt was issued, so a company can refinance its debt at a lower interest rate. However, the presence of the call option makes investors wary about buying it, which tends to increase the effective interest rate at which they will buy the debt. Investor concerns can be mitigated to some extent by providing for a fairly long time period before the issuing company can trigger the call option, and especially if the call price is set somewhat higher than the current market price.

Interest Rate Swaptions

A swaption is an option on an interest rate swap arrangement. The buyer of a swaption has the right, but not the obligation, to enter into an interest rate swap. In essence, a swaption presents the option of being able to lock in a fixed interest rate or a variable interest rate (depending on the terms of the underlying swap arrangement). Thus, a treasurer may suspect that interest rates will begin to rise in the near future, and so enters into a swaption to take over a fixed interest rate. If interest rates do indeed rise, the swaption holder can exercise the swaption. If interest rates hold steady or decline, the swaption is allowed to expire without being exercised.

The two types of swaption are the *payer swaption* and the *receiver swaption*, which are defined as follows:

- *Payer swaption.* The buyer can enter into a swap where it pays the fixed interest rate side of the transaction.
- *Receiver swaption.* The buyer can enter into a swap where it pays the floating interest rate side of the transaction.

There is no formal exchange for swaptions, so each agreement is between two counterparties. This means that each party is exposed to the potential failure of the counterparty to make scheduled payments on the underlying swap. Consequently, it is prudent to only enter into these arrangements with counterparties with high credit ratings or other evidence of financial stability.

Swaption market participants are primarily large corporations, banks, and hedge funds. The most likely counterparty for a corporation is a large bank that has a group specializing in swaption arrangements.

Summary

When reviewing the treasury risk management options outlined in this chapter, pay attention to the level of complexity involved in some of the alternatives. If the company does not have the expertise to engage in transactions involving the more complicated derivatives, do not attempt them; there is a risk of entering into an incorrect derivative transaction, which *increases* a risk rather than reducing it. Instead, work on the less convoluted risk management techniques first, and only enter into more difficult arrangements with proper counseling and oversight. It may be several years before management wants to take on certain derivative arrangements on a regular basis.

Chapter 3
Sales and Marketing Risk Management

Introduction

The marketing department is responsible for building the image of a brand with customers, as well as promoting products and setting price points. As such, it is a key reason why sales may spike or decline, which presents a number of risks to the financial health of a business. In particular, there is a need to use great care in adjusting the brand image that a business projects, as well as the funding of that image. In the following sections, we explore a range of possible risk mitigation activities related to the repositioning of a brand, celebrity spokespersons, false marketing claims, budget cutbacks, product recalls, and similar issues.

Marketing Governance Risk

Marketing may be considered the public face of a company, since the marketing messages that consumers experience are the primary form of identification that they have with a business. As such, it is possible that someone in the department could formulate and release an odd, offensive, or off-target marketing campaign that strikes consumers the wrong way and seriously damages the reputation of the company. The following mitigation techniques can be used to deal with this situation:

- *Centralize marketing.* It is easier to maintain control over the marketing department if it is in one place and under centralized management. This may involve shifting marketing away from subsidiaries, for which there may not be a positive response at the local level.
- *Impose a review.* In a larger business that is constantly running a number of marketing campaigns, it can make sense to require the prior approval of a marketing governance committee that examines each proposed campaign for content and how it fits into the general marketing message of the organization.
- *Use a public relations firm.* An extension of the last point is to hire a public relations firm and task it with reviewing all marketing campaigns prior to their release. This approach is costly, but involves people who have a good idea of the general message that a business wants to send, and who can spot anomalies.

Brand Repositioning Risk

A large amount of time and money goes into the creation of a brand, which is intended to permanently lock a certain quality image in the minds of consumers. Altering a brand image can have catastrophic results if the new image does not "take" with consumers. A possible way to mitigate this risk is to reposition the brand in a distant and less-important market. Doing so allows the marketing staff to make mistakes without undue damage to the brand as a whole.

Celebrity Spokesperson Risk

A company may hire a celebrity as a spokesperson for its brand. This can be a severe problem if the spokesperson subsequently has personal or legal problems that become public knowledge, especially if the person has become closely linked to the brand. In this case, the brand can be significantly damaged. Here are several possible ways to reduce the risk:

- *Rotate celebrities*. The company could move through a series of celebrities on a regular basis, so that the brand benefits from a well-known representative, but does not become so closely intertwined with any one celebrity that the brand image would suffer from the celebrity's issues.
- *Conduct celebrity vetting*. The marketing manager engages in a careful review of all prospective celebrity hires, and only hires those that have absolutely no evidence of issues that could backfire on the firm.
- *Communicate expectations*. Discuss with any prospective hires the behavior that is expected of them, and the consequences of not meeting those expectations.

False Marketing Claims Risk

Competitors routinely monitor the marketing claims of their competitors, and may publicly question the veracity of certain claims. Questions may also come from consumer watchdog groups, government agencies, or investigations arising from lawsuits. It is also possible that a false marketing claim elsewhere in the industry paints a false image with customers of every company in the industry. The following are ways to mitigate this risk:

- *Vet marketing messages*. Have a committee review all marketing messages before they are released, to ensure that all claims made can be substantiated.
- *Vet competitor marketing messages*. Proactively review all marketing messages being used by competitors. If any claim appears to be questionable, ensure that it is not used in the company's own marketing messages. By doing so, the company is protected if the competitor's claim is eventually proven to be false or misleading. Instead, the company can validly state that it has never made that claim.
- *Be a watchdog*. If the industry appears to be unusually susceptible to consumer suspicion about false claims, it may be necessary to police the industry. This means examining competitor claims and privately pointing out to them the dangers to the industry of making excessively aggressive claims.

Advertising Reduction Risk

The marketing department typically has a relatively fixed budget for its advertising expenditures, which tends to be used to fund the same established marketing channels every year. If a sharp cut in this budget is imposed on the department, the marketing staff may impose an across-the-board cut in advertising of all types. If so, there is a risk that sales could sharply decline in an amount greater than the imposed budget reduction. Here are several options to explore that can mitigate the risk of an advertising reduction:

- *Stagger advertising*. Switch between full funding and no funding in consecutive periods on an ongoing basis, and measure the customer response rate in each period. This approach can be used to develop a direct cause-and-effect relationship between advertising and sales, which could be used to attract more funding from management.
- *Eliminate peripheral advertising*. The uses to which the advertising budget has been put in recent years may have become diffused among a broad range of items, perhaps encompassing (for a sports brand) a car racing team, extreme sports, and athlete sponsorships. Sort through these items and completely drop those that appear to give only peripheral support to the brand image being fostered, thereby focusing all funding on core advertising.
- *Experiment*. If the department has not spent time testing the efficacy of its advertising in the past, then now might be a good time to try. Doing so might uncover several nuggets of usable information, such as certain expensive types of advertising triggering minimal brand awareness by consumers. The outcome might be a reshuffling of advertising priorities that can still make the reduced advertising budget effective.

Increased Marketing Cost Risk

The marketing department may be subject to cost pressures from the distribution channels that it uses to send its messages to consumers. For example, the costs to produce television commercials, place radio ads, or send bulk mail may all increase. If so, there are several risk mitigation alternatives available:

- *Test new channels*. The marketing staff should always be testing the cost-benefit of new distribution channels. By doing so, it will be in a better position to reposition funds away from high-cost distribution channels. The best situation is when there are several low-cost alternatives available that have a high customer response rate, and into which the department can quickly shift funds.
- *Double down*. A reverse approach is to pour *more* money into a high-cost distribution channel. This approach can work when there is a high cost-benefit ratio associated with a specific channel, and when the company can obtain volume discounts.

- *Set a threshold.* Some organizations simply accept increased marketing costs each year; they do not impose any structure on the examination of these costs. An alternative is to estimate the threshold cost level above which it is no longer cost-effective to use a specific distribution channel. As the cost approaches this threshold level, the marketing staff can begin to plan for a switch to a different channel. At no point does a business accept distribution costs that have exceeded its threshold level.

Socioeconomic Change Risk

There are many ongoing trends in society that can impact the demand for a product. For example, an emphasis on lower calories may reduce the demand for certain comfort foods, while environmental concerns may drive people away from automobile purchases. As another example, the use of large-screen televisions allows a person to view movies at home, which reduces the demand for viewing at movie theaters. This is a major risk that can significantly counteract the efforts of the marketing department to sell products. The issue is one that senior company management is most responsible for addressing, since it may require that certain product lines be shut down entirely or de-emphasized, while funds are targeted at new products that are intended to be on the leading edge of these societal trends. Still, there are risk mitigation strategies that marketing can employ to reduce the effects of these trends, such as:

- *Refute claims.* One option is to locate studies that refute the claims being made by others to effect change. The intent is to fritter away at the basis for a societal change in the hope that it will die out. The efficacy of this approach tends to be low, since such studies are typically viewed as being paid for by the industry and therefore suspect.
- *Reposition product.* It may be possible to engage in a product reformulation that makes it conform more closely to a societal trend. This is particularly useful if a modest investment can be made in a single product within a product line that pulls up the image of the entire line. For example, the sale of a hybrid car can enhance the image of a car company's entire vehicle lineup.
- *Jump in.* The marketing staff can monitor societal trends and point out to senior management which ones are most likely to require the company to issue entirely new products. If these proposals are funded promptly, the company can have new products well in advance of the competition, and so may even find that its market share has increased.

Product Recall Risk

There may be serious issues with a product that necessitate a recall. This can be a traumatic event from a marketing perspective, since the brand can be severely damaged. It is difficult for the marketing department to engage in risk mitigation activities in this area, since recalls are, by their nature, unforeseen. Still, the following tactics may be of assistance:

- *Monitor complaints*. Invest in a customer complaints database and monitor it frequently, so that problems can be identified as soon as possible. Rapid identification may allow a business to correct a problem during the initial stages of a product rollout, so that the need for a recall is reduced.
- *Create policies*. Work with the senior management team to formulate policies for dealing with product recalls, with the intent of minimizing the negative impact on the company's brands. Policies to consider are:
  - *Authority*. Specifically identify who has the authority to trigger a recall. Doing so reduces the delays and finger-pointing associated with a group decision.
  - *Standard reimbursement*. Formulate a standard response to be given to customers, such as a blanket replacement of the impacted products or a money-back guarantee. This eliminates the delay that would otherwise arise while the management team argues over a response.
  - *Standard response*. Formulate several boilerplate press releases that can address most situations. Doing so eliminates the time that would otherwise be required, with the usual number of iterations as reviews are made by lawyers and public relations consultants.

Incorrect Forecasting Risk

A potentially massive risk is that the sales staff will incorrectly forecast demand for a product, which results in either out-of-stock conditions for popular items or (more likely) excess and potentially obsolete inventory that cannot be sold. This is a particular concern when goods must be ordered well in advance of the selling season, and when there are many variations on the basic product, all of which must be correctly forecasted. Here are a number of options for reducing forecasting risk:

- *Reduce the number of products*. The company may offer so many permutations of the same basic product that it is impossible to reliably forecast demand at the level of the individual inventory item. Instead, deliberately cut back on the number of products offered, to concentrate on a core group that is more easily forecasted.
- *Adopt short production runs*. Use a just-in-time production system that employs fast equipment changeovers, so that production runs can be kept quite short. Doing so eliminates the imperative to employ long production runs that tend to build up excessive amounts of inventory.
- *Shorten the forecast period*. If a just-in-time system is in place (see the preceding item), production can be switched to a different product on short notice, which means that forecasting periods can be reduced. It is much easier to forecast for only a short period of time, so forecasting accuracy should improve.

Customer Loss Risk

Any organization will experience a certain amount of customer churn, where existing customers are replaced by new customers. However, the risk of loss is enhanced when an outgoing customer is quite a large one that accounts for a substantial amount of the organization's total profits. This risk can be mitigated in several ways, including the following:

- *Focus on better mix*. Set a goal of having a larger number of small customers. By doing so, there will be less risk of a profitability decline when customers leave, since no one customer is responsible for most of the company's profits.
- *Access adjacent industries*. If there is no way to sidestep the number of large customers in the targeted industry, it may be time to look elsewhere for a broader mix of customers, such as an adjacent industry. This may involve repositioning the company's products somewhat or altering the sales and marketing focus.
- *Double down*. In some industries, there are only a small number of customers, so any customer loss is catastrophic. In this case, the solution may be to heavily orient the business toward an intense level of customer service. This may involve having a dedicated customer support team for every customer, a management focus on any service failures, and constant customer contact.
- *Offer extended contracts*. The company could offer discounts to its customers in exchange for multi-year contracts, thereby locking in customers for extended periods of time. This option works best when the costs of the seller are expected to decline in the future, so that the cost reductions can be passed along to customers while still preserving reasonable margins.

Contracting Economy Risk

The economy may contract from time to time, which will likely reduce sales or at least curtail the rate of growth. In this environment, it may be necessary to prune sales and marketing costs and wait for the economy to expand again. If the sales and marketing managers do not manage the onset and termination of these contractions and expansions properly, there can be a notable negative financial impact. Here are several ways to mitigate the risk:

- *Monitor leading indicators*. There may be leading indicators that have a history of reliably anticipating the onset of contractions and expansions. If so, monitor them closely, so that there is as much warning as possible of impending changes in consumer demand.
- *Switch focus to existing accounts*. If the company usually suffers severely from a financial contraction, it can make sense to engage in a sharp cutback in marketing to new prospects, and instead focus on increasing sales to existing customers. To do so, prepare a contractionary-phase marketing plan that can be triggered on short notice, and which reorients the sales and marketing employees.

71

Summary

A number of the preceding risk mitigation points revolve around the need to impose a high level of governance and planning on the marketing function. In order to mitigate risks, the marketing staff must exercise great care in examining the messages it projects to customers, while also constantly exploring all possible alternative channels through which it can send its messages. The outcome can be a low-risk environment in which all marketing campaigns adhere closely to a central message, and where the department has a strong grasp of the cost-benefit effects associated with all possible marketing channels.

Chapter 4
Supply Chain Risk Management

Introduction

When an organization outsources a large proportion of its activities or buys a significant part of its total product cost from suppliers, it is likely at great risk of being negatively impacted by changes in its supply chain. For example, commodity prices could increase, supplier factories may be impacted by natural disasters, or strikes could keep deliveries from arriving on time. There are many ways in which to proactively address these issues so that supply chain failures have a reduced impact on a business, or so that some issues can be avoided entirely. The following sections outline these issues and possible solutions.

Supply Chain Risk

The supply chain can be critical to the survival of a business, especially if a large part of the value that a business delivers to its customers actually comes from its suppliers. In these situations, one should evaluate the likelihood of occurrence of each possible supply chain failure, as well as the ability of these failures to disrupt operations. Examples of common supply chain risks to which these analyses can be readily applied are:

- Inadequate supplier performance
- Forecasting errors that lead to shortages or over-investments in purchased goods
- Breakdowns in transportation between suppliers and the company
- Changes in the prices charged by suppliers

The preceding list involves situations that occur with a relatively high degree of frequency, so there is an obvious payback in spending the time to analyze these types of risks. But what about situations in which there could be a major disaster, but only at long intervals? Here are several examples:

- There has been one instance of a river flooding that is adjacent to a supplier's production facility, but the last case was 50 years ago. A 20% increase in the maximum water level would flood the facility.
- A manufacturing facility has been built on an island on the southern fringe of the Caribbean that is well outside of the normal hurricane tracks, but which experienced a Category Two hurricane 15 years ago. During the last occurrence, it took two weeks for the island's government to restore utilities.

- A supplier's headquarters is situated over an earthquake fault that has not shifted in over 100 years. According to historical records, the last earthquake leveled the town in which the building is now situated.
- A major multinational supplier is considering building a production facility in a small country that is currently stable, but which experienced a military take-over two elections ago, followed by a small amount of asset expropriation.

In all of the preceding scenarios, the events are rare enough that it can be difficult to even find detailed historical information about them – and yet there is evidence that a reoccurrence would inflict major damage on the business. A common outcome of these situations is that a proper risk analysis is never completed, since the risk manager is more concerned with events that have much higher frequencies. The result can be epically negative consequences, since there is no contingency in place at all to offset the effects of a major disaster.

A method for dealing with these rare events is to not focus on the probability of occurrence, but rather on the impact of a potential failure in the supply chain. For example, rather than focusing on a minimal probability that a supplier will be shut down due to flood damage, look instead at the impact if that supplier will not be operational for a period of time – irrespective of the cause. A likely outcome is the discovery that the company has planned well for possible shutdowns in deliveries from its high-spend suppliers, but done little to guard against shutdowns elsewhere in its supply chain. For example, a business might maintain large reserve stocks of rare earth minerals for its electronics business because there are so few reliable suppliers, but has completely overlooked its commodity components, which are subject to a different set of risks.

In the market for commodity goods, the main competitive factor is price, which typically leads to rapid industry consolidation as those with the largest and lowest-cost facilities gain market share. The problem with this arrangement from a risk management perspective is that there are very few suppliers remaining, so if a disaster shuts one down, a large part of the total industry capacity has just been eliminated.

Cross-Firm Effects of Supply Chain Disruptions

When a number of companies all buy from a major supplier or group of suppliers located in the same geographic region, this can amplify the negative effects of a supply chain disruption. For example, a major flood shuts down the largest supplier of a certain computer part; because of its production excellence, many major customers order from this supplier. As a result of the shutdown, any of these customers will find that they are in the midst of a broad scramble for alternative supplies, which can greatly increase the cost of replacement parts, while also making it nearly impossible to obtain replacement supplies in a timely manner.

Supply Chain Risk Mitigation Techniques

There are a number of ways in which to reduce the risk of failures in the supply chain, which are only limited by the imagination of the management team. Here are several risk mitigation alternatives:

- *Build inventory reserves*. Maintain additional stocks of inventory that exceed the amounts strictly necessary to maintain the flow of goods through the company's internal production processes, or to ensure that customer stock-out conditions are minimized. This additional safety stock guards against the sudden termination of supplier deliveries. A useful side benefit of a stockpiling program is that it also provides extra stock if there is an unexpected increase in demand.
- *Buy from nearby suppliers*. Shift orders to suppliers located closer to the company or its distribution points, or at least avoid placing orders with the more distant suppliers. Doing so eliminates the risk of in-transit disruptions.
- *Use alternative transport*. It may be possible to arrange for multiple forms of transport, such as by river barge, rail, airplane, and/or truck. By fostering multiple forms of transport, the materials management group gains experience in how to rapidly shift inbound transport when its main form of conveyance is disabled. For example, a truckers' strike may shut down freight hauling on the roads, but still leaves rail transport as a viable alternative.
- *Additional suppliers*. Maintain more than one supplier, and consider using a backup supplier that is located in a different geographic location. By doing so, a disaster that impacts one supplier is less likely to also affect the backup. A variation is to pay a backup supplier to reserve a portion of its capacity, rather than actually placing orders with it on an ongoing basis. The company is then entitled to immediately access this capacity as needed.
- *Encourage additional production sites*. Incentivize suppliers to build additional factories in disparate locations, so that work can continue even in the face of a disaster at one of the locations. The incentives could include low-cost loans to build the extra factories, the promise of a larger share of orders, or outright bonuses.
- *Conduct credit monitoring*. Use such credit research firms as Moody's Analytics and Dun & Bradstreet to monitor the financial health of suppliers. If the credit information forwarded by these research firms indicates a problem, the purchasing department can bolster its planning to ramp up production with secondary suppliers, in anticipation of a default by the primary supplier. This approach can also be used to swap out secondary suppliers that appear to be having financial difficulties. This type of overview can become more detailed if the credit research firms detect a significant problem, perhaps involving an on-site team that investigates the condition of a supplier.
- *Shift production in-house*. If the capital investment is not excessive, it might be economical to produce certain components in-house, rather than outsourcing them to a supplier that is evaluated as being high risk.

- *Develop flexible production facilities*. Develop in-house manufacturing capabilities that can be switched to different production runs without too much difficulty, so that a component shortage from a supplier triggers a move to a different product that does not require the impacted component. However, this is only a short-run solution, since the company will eventually run out of the product that it can no longer manufacture.
- *Hedge prices*. A business may find that its financial results are worse than expected due to a run-up in the prices of its raw materials. The problem can be combatted with hedging arrangements that commit the entity to long-term purchases at the current prices, thereby eliminating the prospect of future price increases. The problem is when the current prices are at historic highs, so the company is committing to keep buying at prices that may subsequently drop. Yes, the hedging will keep the company from paying even higher prices, but the likelihood of a continuing price spiral is probably remote, so the hedging will likely cost the company even more money. Thus, hedging is only profitable in certain circumstances.
- *Redesign products*. A longer-term solution is to redesign products so that the use of certain components is minimized or eliminated. However, it may take an entire product cycle to carry through with this solution.
- *Offer free risk analyses*. A company could offer to send its engineers or an outside consulting group to its suppliers for free, with the intent of identifying risk issues for the suppliers and assisting with their risk mitigation efforts. Doing so eventually results in a more robust supply chain that is less likely to fail.

Project Completion Risk

An organization may be concerned that a supplier cannot complete a major project on time. For example, a company is planning to depart its current premises on June 1, and so needs to have its new corporate headquarters completed by the same date. To mitigate the risk that the new facility will *not* be ready, the company can require the building contractor to post a surety bond. This is a contract guaranteeing that a legal agreement will be completed. It is commonly used to ensure that construction performance is completed. A bond agreement involves the participation of the following three entities:

- *The principal*. This is the party that is supposed to perform in accordance with the requirements of a contract.
- *The obligee*. This is the party receiving the obligation; typically the counter-party to the contract with the principal.
- *The surety*. This is a third party that does not directly perform the requirements of the contract, but rather who guarantees the performance of the principal under the contract.

Thus, a surety bond is a promise to pay the obligee if the principal does not perform under the contract. The surety makes the payment to the obligee. In exchange for this service, the principal pays a fee to the surety for as long as the surety bond is outstanding. In cases where the financial resources of the principal are in doubt, the fee will be quite high, or the surety will insist that all or most of the bond be kept in escrow during the term of the bond.

If there is a claim by the obligee for reimbursement under the surety bond, the surety will investigate the claim, pay it if the claim is valid, and then turn to the principal for reimbursement.

There are several types of surety bonds, including the following:

- *Bid bond.* The principal guarantees that it will enter into an agreement with the obligee if awarded a contract.
- *Performance bond.* The principal guarantees that it will perform the services specified in a contract.

While a surety bond does show that a business has a certain amount of capital, it also acts to block smaller competitors unable to obtain a surety bond from bidding against them. Thus, a surety bond tends to reduce competition among suppliers.

Shifting Risk into the Supply Chain

When a company elects to build products or supply services, it is taking on the risk of changes in the prices of the associated materials or labor. To mitigate this risk, it may be possible to shift work to contractors or subcontractors who are then paid on a fixed-price basis. The result is that the company knows it will incur a fixed amount, with no price variation. This eliminates the risk of a price increase, but also eliminates the potential benefit to be gained from a decline in prices.

The shifting of risk into the supply chain is not free. When faced with a proposal to supply goods or services under a fixed-price arrangement, an experienced contractor or subcontractor will build into the bid price an extra margin that compensates it for the risk of increasing prices.

A company could elect to keep work in-house during periods of falling commodity prices, so that it benefits from the reduced prices, and then outsources during periods of increasing commodity prices, so that this risk is borne by contractors.

Summary

To some extent, supply chain problems originate with the strategy of a business. If the intent of management is to shift more work to suppliers, this introduces all of the risks noted in the preceding sections. The reason for outsourcing more work to suppliers is usually to reduce costs, but this calculation typically does not factor in the increased risks of depending on a supply chain. If risk were factored into the outsourcing decision, it is likely that more work would be retained in-house, or at least that it be outsourced only to local suppliers, where there is less risk of transportation delays.

Chapter 5
Production and Distribution Risk Management

Introduction

One of the main goals driving an effective production and distribution system is to ensure that customers receive quality goods on time. If not, they may cancel their orders or shift their purchases to other suppliers that can fulfill orders more expeditiously. In this chapter, we identify three risks that can interfere with timely deliveries of in-specification goods, and provide possible risk mitigations to all three.

Capacity Failure Risk

A major concern is when the production processes of a business suffer a capacity failure, so that it is unable to deliver the anticipated number of units to customers. This failure reduces sales below expected levels, and also creates an opening for an aggressive competitor to fill the unmet demand with its own products. Here are several ways to mitigate the risk of capacity failure:

- *Manage the bottleneck.* There is probably one key bottleneck in the production process that is the source of capacity failures. If so, identify the bottleneck and then expend extra resources to keep it operating as close to 100% capacity as possible. This may involve paying overtime to run the equipment, keeping maintenance staff permanently situated next to the machine, and so forth.
- *Outsource.* If the company cannot produce additional units without investing in a major expansion, then offload a certain amount of work to a third party, at least for the work that is currently backed up in front of the company's bottlenecked operation.
- *Retain extra capacity.* If the business is subject to spikes in demand, invest in sufficient capacity to meet the high point of the demand spike, rather than just the average level of demand. This can mean retaining older and less-efficient equipment to deal with high-demand situations.
- *Build extra inventory.* If it is too expensive to invest in large amounts of additional capacity, decide whether it is economical to build inventory on an ongoing basis, so that demand spikes can be dealt with from reserve stocks. This decision depends on how quickly inventory spoils or becomes obsolete.

Defective Product Risk

There may be flaws in the production process that result in defective goods being released to the market. For example, components may be produced that are out-of-specification, and which are not detected. This can have a major negative impact on customer perceptions of the business, and could even lead to customer lawsuits or major product recalls. There are several ways to improve upon this situation, including the following:

- *Develop work instructions*. Create complete documentation of every machine setting and procedural step required to manufacture a product to specifications, including allowable tolerances. The documentation should be designed to incorporate how any changes in the various settings and procedures impact each other, so that the sum total of the instructions will result in products that meet specifications. This allows the production staff to correctly set up equipment every time there is an equipment changeover.

- *Conduct an initial batch test*. If the inventory being used is expensive, or if a lengthy production run is contemplated, pause a production line after the first batch has been produced. Test the batch for compliance with customer specifications, and then require a process sign-off by a qualified person. Then continue the production run. This approach is designed to contain the risk of destroying an expensive batch of inventory, and increases the probability of delivering in-specification goods to the customer.

- *Review failures*. Create a team to review the reasons for product failures, and engage in remedial activities to eliminate these issues at the source. If there are many failure problems, create a database that itemizes the types of problems found, resolution status, cost of remediation, and so forth. Also, the team should be comprised of members from the purchasing, engineering, and production departments, since the ultimate cause of failure issues can arise within any of these areas. For example, a failure may be caused by poor-quality raw materials, which must be corrected by the purchasing staff. Or, excessively tight tolerances specified by the engineering department may be causing a large number of products to not meet specifications.

- *Use work cells*. A work cell is a cluster of equipment and personnel that performs a specific task. In this arrangement it is common for a worker to examine each individual part as it arrives at the work cell, to ensure that it is within specifications. This approach turns every work cell into a quality control station, thereby making it much more difficult for faulty products to be released to customers.

- *Use statistical process control*. The production staff measures a selection of work outputs and plots the information on a graph, to see if there are trends in the data. Limit markers are set around the data, indicating the range of outcomes that should be due to natural process variability. If a measurement breaches this marker, it indicates that there is a problem in the process that should be fixed.

- *Install quality review stations*. The preceding activities will detect product flaws throughout the production process. If there are still issues, it may also be necessary to install quality review stations at key points in the production process that conduct a complete examination of each part chosen for review. If problems are detected, it may be necessary to shut down the production line and work through whatever problems have been found.

Loss of Distributor Risk

A key form of product distribution for a manufacturer may be a network of distributors. These distributors maintain inventory at the local level, provide customers with repair and replacement service, and generally act as the local sales network. This approach can save a manufacturer a large amount of sales and service overhead costs. However, there is also a risk that a distributor may elect to take its business elsewhere, in which case the manufacturer immediately loses its sales network in that region, along with the attendant loss of sales. Here are several risk mitigation options:

- *Require due notice.* In the distribution agreement, include a clause that not only requires a distributor to give substantial notice of termination (such as six months), but also to commit to continue servicing customers during the intervening period. Such a clause can be interpreted broadly, but at least improves the probability that the manufacturer will have sufficient time to locate a replacement distributor.
- *Maintain direct sales capability.* Maintain a direct sales capability in at least one sales region, so that the company has a high level of familiarity with the issues involved with direct sales to customers. Then, if necessary, the company can offer direct sales into any region for which a distributor has been lost.
- *Provide additional marketing support.* To make it more attractive to be a distributor of the company, provide additional ongoing marketing funding to distributors. While expensive, this approach will not only attract new distributors, but also make it more worthwhile for existing distributors to stay with the company.

Summary

Of the three risks noted here, the one most likely to impact a business is capacity failure risk. It is quite common to have a bottleneck somewhere in the production process that is limiting the ability of an organization to ship goods quickly. If so, it will be necessary to first locate the bottleneck (which is not always apparent), then ensure that the bottleneck is fully supported with proper maintenance and staffing, and finally to manage the scheduling of production through it to maximize profits. See the author's *Constraint Management* course for more information.

Chapter 6
Human Resources Risk Management

Introduction

The human resources area deals with employee hiring and firing, morale, discrimination, benefits, incentive plans, and other issues that can present unique opportunities and risks for a business. If handled correctly, these activities can result in an environment where turnover is low, employees are hired into positions for which they are well qualified, there is good communication regarding employment issues throughout the business, and employees act in the best interests of the organization. In the following sections, we explore the various risks to which the human resources function is subjected, and how to handle them.

Recruitment Risk

A business may require specific types of skills in order to succeed in its current business or in the development of a new business unit. If the human resources function cannot recruit a sufficient number of qualified people into the required positions, this could hamstring the company's operations. In some organizations, the ability to recruit key positions may even be considered *the* constraint on company operations. For example, a consulting firm may specialize in providing people to a major government defense agency, but only if they already have a top secret clearance. These people may be in great demand, while the number of clearances granted places a hard cap on the number of potential recruits in the marketplace.

There are a number of ways in which to maximize the ability of an organization to recruit personnel, including the following:

- *Add a human resources department.* Many organizations treat the human resources department as just a transaction processing function that arranges for benefits and handles hiring and firing paperwork. This approach may not work when recruiting is a bottleneck, since line managers cannot allocate enough time to the task. If so, hire a large enough human resources staff to yield a concentrated hiring effort.
- *Offer employee bonuses.* Expand the pool of potential candidates by offering a substantial bonus to employees if they can bring in candidates that are then hired by the company and remain with the firm for a certain period of time.
- *Require management networking.* Increase the number of potential candidates by making networking with candidates a required function of management positions. Doing so results in candidates being accessed who may not even be looking for jobs.

- *Target a higher pay level*. The most obvious risk mitigation effort is to increase pay levels for the designated positions. This approach can also be used for those already hired by the company, to minimize losses to competitors. However, there is a risk of inciting a bidding war for key talent.
- *Offer a richer benefits package*. Examine the benefits packages of competitors and offer improvements in key areas, such as higher pension plan matching, more tuition reimbursement, and longer vacation periods.
- *Issue offers faster*. Some companies have lengthy recruiting processes that require candidates to repeatedly return for more interviews. Consider accelerating the process, so that candidates can be given offers within the shortest possible time frame. If coupled with a high pay level, this can pull recruits off the market before competitors have a chance to interview them.
- *Train in-house*. Depending on the skill level required, it can make sense to train existing employees into the required positions. This may work best when the training period is not excessive. A possible downside is that fully-trained employees will then go elsewhere, so this approach may also require a pay boost to lock in employees.

A number of the preceding items have considerable costs attached to them. To mitigate the recruitment and retention cost, it will be necessary to closely define which positions are both needed and difficult to fill, so that the extra funding is only spent on these positions. Otherwise, a company could use a shotgun approach to spend inordinate sums for *all* personnel, rather than for just targeted positions.

Incorrect Hire Risk

There is a major risk associated with making an incorrect hire. Depending on the position, someone hired with the wrong skill set, interpersonal skills, or motivations could play havoc within a business. In a worst-case scenario, an incorrect hire could commit a major fraud, potentially taking down an entire business. There are several ways to detect whether a recruit might not be the correct person for a position, including:

- *Require background checks*. Conduct a mandatory background check prior to making job offers. These investigations may uncover instances of fraud, firings, drug use, or criminal activity.
- *Impose testing*. There are a number of tests that job candidates can take that measure a variety of aptitudes. These tests are not only beneficial for the employer; they may also keep a job candidate away from an unsuitable position.
- *Conduct a professional evaluation*. For managerial and key specialist positions, a company may require candidates to have a discussion with a psychologist, who writes a report for management that evaluates each candidate's suitability for a position.

Downsizing Risk

When a business finds it necessary to downsize the workforce, there is a significant risk that those key performers still remaining will be more likely to find work elsewhere, while a general decline in morale is also possible that will sap productivity. The following activities can mitigate these risks:

- *Clarify the downsizing.* There should be a well-defined process for determining who is to be let go, such as by the seniority of employees. By acting consistently, employees will know how at risk they may be in the event of future layoffs, and so can decide whether they should start looking for a new employer.
- *Minimize work environment impact.* A key consideration when downsizing is how it will impact the work environment. A deep across-the-board cutback is virtually guaranteed to crush any residual morale, since the remaining staff will be scrambling to preserve their jobs and working through the immense backlog of work that they must now handle with fewer resources. To mitigate these effects, communicate constantly with the staff and try to accommodate their needs whenever possible (such as allowing flex hours). Also, consider paring away entire business units, rather than spreading cuts across the organization. Doing so makes a downsizing essentially unnoticeable to most employees.
- *Be decisive.* There is nothing more agonizing for the staff than to suffer through an ongoing series of downsizings, since a high level of uncertainty permeates the work environment. Instead, management should act decisively to complete the entire downsizing at one time, so that the remaining employees can put the upheaval behind them as fast as possible.
- *Offer a hire-back bonus.* If there is an expectation that business will eventually pick back up, and if the people to be laid off have significant skills, it may make sense to offer them a bonus if they are hired back. The advantage of doing so is that employees may be more willing to subsist on temporary work until they are hired back. Of course, convincing employees to wait around in this manner requires a sufficiently large hire-back bonus to grab their attention.

Worsening Employee Morale Risk

A company may operate in such a high-pressure environment that employees are under a great deal of stress, which can negatively impact their morale. This can have a number of side-effects that can damage the business, such as worsening customer service, higher employee turnover, and employee unwillingness to work overtime. There are several ways to deal with this risk, such as:

- *Overstaff.* When the training period for a position is relatively short or the number of available job candidates is high, consider hiring somewhat in advance of actual needs, so that there are more than enough staff available to complete tasks.

- *Allow flex hours*. Allow employees to move their working hours around a few core hours during which they must be working, to accommodate their personal needs. This approach is especially useful when workers are trying to avoid the prime commuting hours, or need to drop off or pick up children at school.

- *Communicate*. Regularly discuss with employees those issues that can potentially cause morale problems, and what the company is doing to mitigate these issues. This is especially useful when remediation activities may require a long period of time, so that employees understand the time scale required to improve the situation.

Discrimination Risk

Some or all of the members of the management team may be laying the groundwork for legal claims against the business if their actions appear to be discriminatory. These actions could include unjustified preferences in promotional decisions, excessive disciplinary actions, and the denial of overtime pay. If discrimination can be proven to have been applicable to a large number of employees, a business could find itself liable for a substantial settlement. Consequently, several mitigating activities should be considered, including the following:

- *Conduct awareness training*. Periodically review discrimination issues with the management team, and particularly in regard to recent cases within the business and the legal liabilities of the organization in this area. Setting up these reviews as an ongoing process keeps the issue in front of the management team.

- *Track minority positions*. Identify the proportions of minority positions within each job classification currently employed by the company. This information can be used to spot holes in the classifications where minorities are underrepresented.

- *Fast track complaints*. No matter how well the management team may think it is dealing with discrimination issues, there may still be complaints related to unaddressed areas of the company. Employees should be encouraged to forward their issues directly to the human resources department, which is then authorized to fast track an investigation and remediation activities. This approach improves the employee perception that discrimination will not be tolerated.

Position Misclassification Risk

It is possible that the company has been mis-classifying certain positions as being exempt when they are actually non-exempt. This means that the company should have been paying overtime to certain employees, perhaps for a long time. If so, it could be liable for substantial fines by the Department of Labor, and is also liable for the amount of this back pay.

The Department of Labor issues guidelines for what types of positions are considered to be exempt. The general classifications of exempt positions are:

- *Executive employee.* A person who manages the enterprise, supervises at least two full-time employees, and has the authority to hire and fire employees. An example is the vice president of sales.
- *Administrative employee.* A staff position where the primary duty is to perform office or non-manual work directly related to the operations of the employer. These employees exercise discretion and independent judgment. An example is a due diligence analyst.
- *Professional employee.* Performs work that requires advanced knowledge in the fields of science or learning, as well as the exercise of discretion and judgment. An example is a doctor. A variation on this designation is the creative professional, who engages in work requiring invention, imagination, originality or talent in a field of artistic or creative endeavor. An example is a choreographer.
- *Computer employee.* A person employed as a computer systems analyst, computer programmer, software engineer, or a similar position.
- *Outside salesperson.* A person whose primary duty is to generate sales, and who is customarily engaged away from the premises of the employer.

Someone who is paid wages receives a pay rate per hour, multiplied by the number of hours worked. A person who receives wages is also entitled to overtime pay of 1.5 times his normal rate of pay if he works more than 40 hours per week. This person is considered to be non-exempt, which means he or she is covered by the overtime pay requirements contained within the Fair Labor Standards Act.

Only those positions that are clearly exempt from overtime payments should be designated as salaried. This means that any new job descriptions must be carefully reviewed to ensure that the correct designation is applied. Consider bringing in a labor law specialist to examine the pay status of all employees, to ensure that compensation designations are correct.

Inflated Benefits Cost Risk

Benefits costs that continually spiral upward can be a major financial risk, especially in a business where employee retention calls for a strong benefits package. Here are a number of ways in which to mitigate the risk:

Aggregation Techniques

- *Form a purchasing coalition.* It may be possible for several organizations to create a coalition for the purchase of benefits. By creating a larger pool of employees, they can obtain better rates from benefit providers. However, doing so may require that some overhead costs be incurred to manage the coalition, as well as a commitment to remain in the coalition for a certain minimum period of time.

- *Bundle benefits.* Consider shifting a large bundle of benefits to a single service provider. By doing so, the increased volume of business should entitle the company to lower fees. For example, payroll service providers also offer 401(k) plan administration services, while some medical insurance providers also provide other types of insurance. The main downside of bundling is that some plans favored by employees may be dropped when benefits are shifted into a bundled arrangement.
- *Aggregate subsidiaries.* A company may have a number of subsidiaries, each with its own benefits plan. If so, centralize benefits administration and require all subsidiaries to use the same benefit providers. By aggregating the number of employees using a smaller number of benefit plans, the company may obtain better benefit pricing. This concept may not work for outlying company locations where benefit coverage is not available from a selected provider, but could still be implemented for other company locations.

Benefit Swaps

- *Swap time off for benefits.* If employees do not have a need for certain benefits, encourage them to take other benefits in exchange that are less costly to the company. For example, a younger person may feel that life insurance is not necessary, and so may be willing to swap it for an extra day off, perhaps even at a reduced rate of pay.
- *Swap lower drug co-pay for generic purchases.* Generic drugs are much less expensive than name-brand formulations, so offer employees a lower co-pay if they buy generic drugs.
- *Swap lower drug co-pay for mail order purchases.* When employees have long-term prescriptions, the most cost-effective way to fill these prescriptions is to assign them to a mail-order operation that mails the drugs at regular intervals, and at lower cost than the neighborhood pharmacy. To encourage the use of mail-order prescription fulfillment, offer a lower co-pay to employees if they use this service. In essence, the company is swapping a portion of the co-pay for a lower overall drug cost.

Benefit Limitations

- *Cap the benefit offered.* Some benefits are guaranteed to increase as employees stay with the company for longer periods of time. For example, the costs of life insurance and disability insurance will increase as employees become older and their base compensation increases. For these types of benefits, the company could establish a maximum benefit amount that it is willing to pay, over which employees must pay the remaining benefit cost. The primary downside is that the cost differential paid by employees may eventually become so great that they drop certain benefits entirely.

- *Only provide coverage to employees.* A smaller business with limited funding might opt to just offer benefits to its employees. All dependents would be excluded from coverage. This approach is more common in businesses that are scaling up their operations, and intend to provide more comprehensive coverage once their cash flow improves.
- *Pay cash for benefits.* The company could issue a fixed cash amount to its employees as part of their ongoing compensation, which is designated as payment for benefits. Employees are then responsible for obtaining any type of benefits they want with this cash. The company can direct employees to a list of benefit providers from which they can purchase benefit packages. This approach completely caps the amount of benefits expense that a business will pay, because all risk of benefit inflation, as well as administrative chores, are shifted to employees. This is not a very employee-friendly approach, but could work in situations where a very young work force is more interested in receiving extra cash than in receiving benefits.
- *Terminate cash-out option.* If the company allows employees to demand a cash payment for any unused sick time, this policy merely encourages them to work through situations when they are sick and should be home, thereby infecting their co-workers and causing more sickness. Consequently, do not offer payment for unused sick time to employees.
- *Limit vacation carryovers.* When employees are allowed to carry over their vacation hours to later years, this means that the company will eventually have to pay them for the vacation hours at the (presumably) higher rate of pay in existence when the vacation hours are eventually used. It also calls for the recordation of a vacation liability on the company's balance sheet that will carry over for however long employees do not use their vacation hours. To mitigate this liability, require employees to use their accrued vacation time within a certain period of time, or only allow a small carryover into the next year. However, be aware that this restriction may cause employees to take vacation at the end of the year, when their services may be quite urgently needed. Also, it may be illegal to impose a "use it or lose it" rule where vacation time is cancelled if not used, since vacation time is considered an earned benefit that cannot be taken away.

Benefit Reductions and Cost Sharing

- *Expand plan after initial service period.* If the company experiences a large amount of employee turnover, it may make sense to offer only a basic level of benefits during the first year or two of employment, after which employees are eligible for a more comprehensive set of benefits. Dangling richer benefits in front of new employees may also create an incentive for them to stay with the company, thereby reducing turnover. The same approach can be used with accrued vacation, where there is a significant increase in the amount of vacation accrual after an employee has worked for the company for at least one or two years.

- *Require co-pays*. Require employees to pay a high co-pay for a variety of benefits, such as for prescriptions, doctor visits, and hospitalizations. The theory is that higher co-pays will prevent employees from seeking treatment for minor ailments, thereby reducing the total amount of medical bills. However, high co-pays may also prevent employees from seeking treatment in the early stages of an illness, resulting in vastly higher expenses later, when they are in much worse condition. Consequently, co-pays should not be set at inordinately high levels.
- *Require cost sharing*. The company can require employees to take on a larger share of the cost of any type of benefit. For example, it may be possible to shift from requiring 10% employee payments for medical insurance to 30%. The same approach may be applied to dental insurance, disability insurance, and life insurance. By shifting an increased amount of costs to employees, it is also more likely that some coverage will eventually be moved to the benefits plan of a spouse. However, this approach can be taken too far. It may result in lower-wage employees having to back out of coverage entirely, if they cannot afford their share of the costs. It can also be a problem when a recruit is comparing the benefit plans of possible employers, since a lower cost-sharing percentage may lead to a decision to work for a competitor.

The exact mix of the preceding activities that should be used will be based on the demographics of the employees and what they perceive to be critical benefits. Consequently, the risk of inflating benefits costs must be dealt with differently by each employer.

Increased Unemployment Rate Risk

The unemployment taxes that state governments charge to employers can increase dramatically, depending on the number of employees that an employer has laid off or fired in the past calendar year. This increase can substantially increase payroll costs, and so can be considered a moderate financial risk. There are several ways to mitigate the risk of an increased unemployment rate, including the following:

- *Cut back hours in general*. When a business downturn is expected to be relatively short, impose a general reduction in hours worked on the entire workforce, rather than laying off anyone. Doing so can dramatically reduce the unemployment charges against a company's account with the state.
- *Staff for average demand levels*. Only employ full-time staff to meet average customer demand. When demand spikes, bring in temporary workers to meet the extra demand, and let them go as soon as demand drops back down. This approach minimizes the need for layoffs.

Performance Incentive Plan Risk

When an organization rolls out a new performance incentive plan, there is a risk that its provisions will incentivize employees to behave in ways that are detrimental to the business. For example, a bonus plan that pays employees based on sales growth may trigger sales of items that have low profit margins, so that the profitability of the organization suffers. This is a difficult risk to mitigate; here are several suggestions for doing so:

- *Make gradual changes.* Rather than imposing a radically new incentive plan on employees, consider targeting a revised plan that will be achieved in a few years, and make gradual changes to the annual plan in order to eventually arrive at the revised plan. Doing so allows management to monitor the behavior of employees as different facets of the new plan are rolled out.
- *Conduct a pilot test.* If the company is large enough to have several similar subsidiaries, consider conducting a pilot test at just one of them, and observe the outcome for a reasonable period of time to see if employee behavior is changing as expected.
- *Hire a consultant.* Have an expert in incentive plans review every proposed plan, and provide advice regarding possible plan outcomes. This individual should have seen the outcomes of many similar plans, and so can estimate the impact on employees.

It is possible that a performance incentive plan will trigger employee behavior that increases the level of risk. For example, there may be a hefty year-end bonus if profits surpass a certain target figure. If so, employees will be tempted to engage in high-risk activities in order to achieve the bonus. To avoid this sort of behavior, alter the incentive plan to focus on more long-range results that take risk into account. For example:

- Pay in stock options that vest over a multi-year period
- Apply a claw-back provision (taking back a bonus) if losses occur at a later date that are driven by current activities
- Adjust bonuses based on an analysis of the risk mitigation activities of a targeted individual

Accidents Risk

Depending on the type of work environment, an organization could be at significant risk of having its employees injured on the job. Some jobs may normally involve hazardous activities (such as mining or logging), or employees may be involved in construction or transport activities where there is an enhanced risk of injury. There are multiple risks for a business that arise from employee accidents, including lawsuits, strikes, increases in the cost of workers' compensation insurance, and declining employee morale. It may not be possible to entirely eliminate the risk of accidents, but here are several suggestions for reducing their number:

- *Identify causes*. Note the exact cause of each accident and have a safety expert develop a safeguard. This may involve, for example, the use of guard rails, safety fencing, warning signs, and the removal of obstructions.
- *Provide training*. If new employees will be working in a hazardous environment, provide them with detailed training that is reinforced during a probationary period. When there are changes to the work environment, ensure that all employees working in the area are given appropriate training.
- *Enforce safety procedures*. Some employees may ignore standard safety procedures. If so, discipline them with increasing levels of rigor, with the specific goal of enforcing safety standards.
- *Maintain equipment*. Some equipment can be dangerous if it fails, so adopt a schedule of preventive maintenance and ensure that it is completed in a timely manner. Further, if employees report malfunctioning equipment, give it a high priority in the maintenance department's work queue.

OSHA Violations Risk

The Occupational Safety and Health Administration (OSHA) enforces a number of regulations regarding workplace safety. If a company is not cognizant of these regulations, it could be liable for substantial OSHA fines. To mitigate this risk, hire an experienced workplace safety consultant who has a detailed knowledge of OSHA regulations, and implement any recommendations made by this person.

Human Resources Activities to Mitigate Risk

The human resources department can become proactively involved in risk management by participating in several activities, rather than reacting to the risk profiles of different scenarios arising elsewhere in the business. These activities include:

- *Identify issues during interviews*. Interviewers can probe job candidates about how they deal with risk. Those that prove to be quite risk averse might be rejected, while those able to incorporate risk assessments into their decisions could be more likely to receive a job offer. By screening for risk aptitude early on, an organization can reduce the probability that its employees will make incorrect risk decisions in the future.
- *Identify issues during exit interviews*. Employees who decide to leave the company may do so because they have identified risks within the business and then been ignored when they tried to have the issues rectified. They may be more willing to discuss these issues during an exit interview, so the human resources staff should specifically bring this up as a standard exit interview question.
- *Impose risk training*. The department can conduct training in which employees deal with different scenarios, to show them how to identify risky situations and manage them correctly.

Summary

Risk management in the human resources area is especially important in certain types of industries where the chief constraint on growth is the ability to hire qualified personnel, and especially when the organization provides services to customers. In these situations, the compensation, benefits, and work environment of an entity must be carefully structured in order to maximize its ability to add staff, minimize turnover, incentivize employees, and avoid penalties. The management of these risks must be continually re-evaluated as the labor environment of a firm changes.

Chapter 7
Accounting Risk Management

Introduction

Risks in the accounting area might be considered to only encompass errors in recording transactions and producing financial statements – which can certainly cause enough trouble by themselves. However, there are additional areas within the sphere of influence of the company controller that can also present unique risks, such as budgeting errors, overspending, due diligence mistakes, and public company disclosures. All of these issues are noted in the following sections.

Financial Statement Error Risk

There is a possibility that the accounting department will make a material error in the creation of an organization's financial statements. This may be caused by a mis-interpretation of the accounting standards or by the incorrect recordation of a transaction. In either case, the result is a financial statement error that must be re-stated. An error of this type can negatively impact investor confidence, which can have several additional ramifications. First, it can lead to the ouster of some members of the management team, though this usually only occurs if the error is an egregious one. Second (and more likely), it can lead to a decline of investor confidence in the financial results being reported, which triggers their sale of company stock, and therefore a decline in the share price.

Risk mitigation for financial statement errors can involve several activities, including the following:

- *Enforce a closing procedure*. The accounting staff should always follow a checklist of closing activities, so that no closing activities are missed. Such a list is described in the author's *Closing the Books* course.
- *Involve auditors*. When the accounting staff is dealing with a new type of business transaction, contact the company's auditors and discuss the most appropriate way to account for it. Then document this methodology and run it by the auditors again to ensure that they approve of how the transaction will be dealt with.
- *Initiate a feedback loop*. Maintain a log of all accounting recordation errors found, and ensure that each one is dealt with, such as by using enhanced training, better procedures, or shifting the work to a more qualified employee.

Tax Return Error Risk

The preparation of an entity's income tax return may be in error, or the decision is made to take an aggressive tax position that is later struck down by the Internal Revenue Service. In either case, the business may be liable for substantial penalties and fines.

In the first case, where a tax return is in error, a business can take multiple risk mitigation steps, such as outsourcing to a qualified tax preparer, requiring a review by a second tax preparer, and logging all tax preparation issues as they occur in order to take procedural and training mediation steps.

The latter situation, where an aggressive tax position is taken, is a deliberate action taken by management, where the rewards of a reduced or deferred tax payment are weighed against the risk of penalties and fines. This means that management should already be cognizant of the risk, and has decided to accept the risk.

Budgeting Error Risk

One of the riskiest areas in a business relates to the corporate budget, and especially when the document is closely integrated into the operations and performance systems of a business. A budget presents a view of the future, and if the assumptions used in the budget model are wrong, then this view can be dangerously misleading. Among the many budget-related risks are the following:

- *Revenue estimates*. Perhaps the most egregious error in a budget is the excessive optimism of senior management in setting a very high sales target for the coming year. This presents the risk of then spending too much on infrastructure to support sales that never appear. This risk can be mitigated by adopting a severely questioning attitude about the veracity of additional increments of sales. Another possibility is to use periodic milestone reviews during the budget year to see if actual sales are keeping pace with projections; if not, dial back the corresponding budgeted expenditures to match actual sales.
- *Pacing assumptions*. A major potential error not built into the budget is a realistic pace at which a business can expand. For example, the average salesperson may be able to sell $1,000,000 per year, so a budgeted increase of $8,000,000 mandates that eight additional salespeople be hired before the budget year begins. At a more nuanced level (using the same example), one should also assume that a new salesperson cannot sell as well as a more experienced salesperson, and also that a salesperson added to an existing territory will be left with fewer choice customers, and so will sell even less. The in-depth examination of the drivers behind a change in growth can result in much tighter control over this risk.
- *Profit assumptions*. Increases in sales may assume that the company can continue to earn its historical margins on sales. However, the original market niches may be tapped out, which will force the enterprise into new niches for which the associated margins may be quite different. If so, additional

complexity must be added to the model to account for the best estimates of how margins will change in each new niche.

- *Bottleneck management*. There is a constraint somewhere in most organizations that prevents sales from increasing. Perhaps it is the lack of an experienced sales force, a design team that cannot create new products in a timely manner, or production equipment that is already operating at capacity. Whatever the reason may be, the existence of this bottleneck must be acknowledged in the budget by expending funds to bypass or supplement the item in question. If not, management may find that there is a rigid cap on the sales level of the business.

There are two major ways to mitigate the risk associated with budgeting. They are:

- *Model multiple scenarios*. Most organizations only develop a single version of the budget year, which represents the median estimate of the management team regarding what will transpire. A single budget model ignores all outlier events, some of which are bound to occur during the year. As an alternative, consider using a simplified model to observe how the results of the business would change if any one or a combination of several outlier events occurs. For example, model for the loss of a major customer, the marketplace rejection of a new product, or the shutdown of a subsidiary. An analysis of several variations on the budget can lead the management team to be more careful in the size and placement of its funding bets.
- *Engage in ongoing reviews and updates*. The difference between the budget model and actual results will likely diverge to an increasing extent over the course of the year, to the point where actions taken in accordance with the budget plan are not even remotely helpful to the ongoing competitiveness of the business. This effect can be mitigated by engaging in frequent reviews and updates of the budget model. It may even be possible to have no budget at all, instead relying upon a summary-level forecast that is updated once a month. See the author's *Budgeting* course for more information about how to operate without a budget.

Overpayment Risk

It is possible that a supplier invoice will be paid more than once, and cannot be recovered from the recipient. This risk applies to both suppliers and employees. Examples are:

- A supplier sends an invoice that is not paid on time, so it sends a copy of the invoice as a reminder. The company then pays both invoices – the original and the copy.
- A payroll clerk is preparing the final check for a departing employee, and overpays the amount of unused vacation time. Since the person then leaves the company, there is no way to recover the funds.

- An employee asks for an advance on her wages, and then leaves the company before it is paid back.

Of the issues noted here, the largest risk in terms of severity is likely to be a duplicate payment to a supplier. Excessive employee payments tend to be much smaller.

The risk of overpayment can be mitigated through the application of several internal controls, though there may remain some risk of overpayment for a few outlier transactions. Possible mitigation options are:

- Use a software feature that flags all duplicate invoices entered into the system.
- Make sure that there is only one vendor record for each supplier, so that duplicate invoices are not paid through a separate record, which would circumvent the duplicate invoice flagging feature.
- Institute a standard policy for entering invoice numbers in a consistent manner (such as not using leading zeros), so that the resulting invoice numbers can be more readily flagged by the software as being duplicate invoices.
- Institute a policy of not allowing any employee advances; instead, employees are directed to a local bank for a loan application.
- Install a computerized employee time tracking system (perhaps using badge swipes), so that hours worked are automatically accumulated and paid.

Overspending Risk

A common enough issue is for spending to exceed revenues with little control over the amount spent. The result is spiraling losses or at least a situation in which increasing sales do not correspond to the expansion of profits. There are many ways to reduce this risk, including the following:

- *Set a management example.* If the management team sets a frugal example, this will trickle down throughout the business, making it easier to impose tight cost controls everywhere.
- *Identify discretionary spending.* At the most minimal level of control, identify which costs are not essential in the short-term to the operation of the business. Examples of these costs are expenditures for repairs, advertising, and training. Continuing to avoid these expenditures for a long period of time will damage an organization, but they can be avoided briefly.
- *Enforce the budget.* The accounting staff can issue budget-versus-actual reports to the company, and the purchasing staff can refuse to issue purchase orders if a department head exceeds the budgeted amount. This can cause problems, especially in environments where the organization must continually react to competitive pressures on short notice, and so must be able to expend funds, irrespective of the budget.
- *Issue responsibility reports.* Management should assign responsibility to someone in the company for every expense line item in the income statement. The accounting department then issues reports to each of the responsible

parties, noting in detail the expenditures made to date for which they are responsible.

Use Tax Risk

A risk whose outcome is usually more annoying than life threatening is the prospect of unexpectedly having to pay use taxes. Use taxes are the same as sales taxes, but they are paid by the buyer of goods and services when this function is not fulfilled by the seller. A great many organizations ignore the requirement to pay use taxes, and so are forced to pay these amounts, along with fines and penalties, when they are audited by the applicable government.

When a business elects not to remit use taxes, it is effectively accepting the risk of later paying for the taxes as the result of a use tax audit. If it is not aware of this requirement and is then audited, then continuing noncompliance after this initial notification represents a management decision to accept the risk. If the size of a use tax audit billing is large enough to focus the attention of management, it may instead direct the controller to conduct a monthly review of use tax liabilities, and make these payments when due.

Due Diligence Error Risk

The accounting staff may be called upon to conduct due diligence on the accounting records and financial statements of a potential acquiree. There is a significant possibility that this analysis will either miss or misinterpret key accounting issues, which could lead to significant losses if the company goes through with the acquisition as a result of a favorable report from the accountants.

Due diligence is a high-risk area, for several reasons. First, the accounting staff is typically under pressure to complete its analysis within a short period of time. Second, the accounting personnel are being asked to conduct this review in addition to their regular responsibilities, and so cannot devote their full attention to the task. And finally, they are not trained in due diligence, which is more of an auditing function than an accounting function.

There are several ways to deal with due diligence error risk, all of which involve a much higher expenditure on analysis work than using the company's accounting staff. Management must weigh the added cost of the following alternatives against the reduced risk of missing key due diligence findings. The options are:

- Maintain a separate in-house staff that is trained in due diligence work. This group has no other responsibilities, understands auditing, and has experience with prior due diligence efforts, and so will conduct a much better analysis. This option works best for a serial acquirer.
- Hire outside auditors, attorneys, and valuation experts to conduct a detailed analysis of the potential acquiree. These people are specialists in due diligence analysis, but will charge by the hour, so their total cost can be substantial. There is also a tendency for them to dig too deep into picayune matters in

order to increase their billings. This option works best for an occasional acquirer that cannot justify having an in-house due diligence staff.

Fraud Risk

Fraud is a deception intended to result in personal gain. There are two major types of fraud, which are the loss of assets and the intentional misstatement of the financial statements. Most fraudulent activities result in losses that are immaterial to the financial well-being of a business, and so represent a relatively small risk. However, a few of these events can involve massive losses, and so must be considered key risks that require constant defensive attention.

There are many ways in which fraud can be accomplished, and hundreds of controls may be used to prevent it. Rather than delving into the details of these preventive measures, we mention general types of activities that are used to mitigate the risk of fraud. They are:

- *Process controls*. When any accounting or treasury system is installed, a controls specialist should be involved in the design of the system. This person inserts controls into the system that are designed to block someone from engaging in fraud.
- *Change control*. The forms and processes of a business will change on a regular basis to meet the needs of business partners, new accounting requirements, new systems, and so forth. Whenever these changes occur, existing controls may be lost and replacement controls may not be added. A controls specialist should review these system changes and insert or adjust controls as appropriate.
- *Policies and procedures*. All of the key accounting and treasury processes of a business should be fully documented, including descriptions of all work steps, responsible parties, applicable policies, and forms. Doing so provides structure to systems, thereby reducing the risk of changes being made that could give someone the opportunity to commit fraud.
- *Internal audits*. Have an internal group of well-trained auditors examine all company processes on a rotating basis, focusing in particular on those areas that present the greatest risk of fraud. This group should report to the audit committee of the board of directors, so that the management team is not in a position to influence the reports and recommendations of this group.
- *External auditor commentary*. The procedures of a company's external auditors are not explicitly designed to detect fraud, but they may note certain control issues as part of their investigations. These issues are usually summarized in a recommendations letter at the end of each audit. Peruse this letter and make adjustments to the company's controls as necessary.

The preceding points will not eliminate fraud, but they can make it considerably more difficult for someone to succeed in pulling off fraud of material proportions.

Public-Company Risks

There are a number of issues that arise when a company has its shares publicly traded. For example, a periodic filing with the Securities and Exchange Commission (SEC) might be incorrect, which may lead to fines or shareholder lawsuits. Or, if the share price of the business drops too low, it could be delisted from a stock exchange. Another possibility is that a hostile acquirer could buy enough publicly-available shares to acquire a controlling interest in the business. To some extent, these issues are simply part of the public company environment. However, there are some risk mitigation possibilities, such as:

- *Form a disclosure committee*. A disclosure committee must formally review and approve all press releases and SEC filings before they are issued, with a specific mandate to look for incorrect or inadequate reporting. At a minimum, an experienced securities attorney should conduct this review.
- *Engage in investor relations*. Maintain an active investor relations function, which conducts road shows, earnings calls, and investor meetings, and also issues press releases to maximize the amount of information in the marketplace. Doing so reduces the risk of share price variation that can be caused by investor uncertainty.
- *Develop a company story*. Create a clear story regarding the company's mission and reinforce it with related strategic and tactical actions, so there is little investor uncertainty regarding what the company is doing.
- *Require management participation*. Include the most experienced and presentable members of the management team in investor activities (such as an investor day), so that investors can gain confidence in the depth and experience of the management team as a whole.

The SEC requires that a publicly held business report in its annual Form 10-K report a thorough listing of all risks that the organization may experience. The intent is to warn investors of what could reduce the value of their investments in the company. The following sample disclosure reveals the extent of this reporting:

SAMPLE DISCLOSURE

You should carefully consider the following risks and all of the other information set forth in this report. If any of the events or developments described below actually occurs, our business, financial condition, and results of operations may suffer. In that case, the trading price of our common stock may decline and you could lose all or part of your investment.

Some of the risks related to the business include:

- *Affiliate control*. Members of Ninja's Board of Directors and its executive officers, together with their affiliates, own a significant number of shares of Ninja outstanding common stock. Accordingly, these stockholders, if they act together, can have significant control over matters requiring approval of company stockholders, including the election of directors and approval of significant corporate transactions. The concentration of ownership, which could result in a continued concentration of representation on the Board of Directors, may delay, prevent or deter a change in control and could deprive stockholders of an opportunity to receive a premium for their common stock as part of a sale of our assets. Ninja's directors, executive officers and other affiliates will continue to exert significant control over the company's future direction, which could reduce its future sale value.

- *Customer concentrations.* In the commercial chef market, sales to large restaurant chains comprise a significant proportion of total company sales. The termination of sales to Ninja's five largest restaurant chain customers would eliminate 35% of that segment's total sales. The company cannot be certain that current customers will continue to purchase from it.

- *Dividends.* The company has never declared or paid any cash dividends or distributions on its common stock and intends to retain future earnings, if any, to support operations and to finance expansion. Therefore, the company does not anticipate paying any cash dividends on the common stock in the foreseeable future.

- *Funding availability.* Given the state of the current credit markets, it may be difficult to obtain funds for either operational needs or prospective acquisitions. Ninja currently has $3 million of debt funding available through a previously authorized loan from Fourth National Bank. The company's next-year budget projects sufficient cash requirements to use all but $500,000 of the available debt funding.

- *Growth strategy.* Ninja's growth strategy involves expanding into additional foreign markets. The company's ability to do so may be negatively impacted by the need to work with foreign partners, as well as to sell into markets where there may be currency restrictions. There may also be cases in which vigorous local competition from existing businesses could impede Ninja's ability to gain any significant market share.

- *Industry trends.* The company derives a large part of its revenue from customers in the commercial restaurant business. As a result, Ninja's business, financial condition, and results of operations depend upon the conditions and trends affecting this industry. For example, a decline in consumer spending could lead restaurant chains to reduce their spending on kitchen supplies, which would reduce Ninja's sales.

- *Patent protection.* The patent protecting the company's use of carbon blade knives will expire in 20X9. At that time, competitors may use the same technology to create their own knife blades, which could result in extensive price competition. If so, the company's margins on the sale of this product will likely decline.

- *Personnel loss.* The future success of the company depends in part on the continued service of the executive officers and other key management, sales, and operations personnel, and on the company's ability to continue to attract, motivate, and retain additional highly qualified employees. The loss of the services of one or more of these people, or the company's inability to recruit replacements for them or to otherwise attract, motivate, or retain qualified personnel could have an adverse effect on the business, its operating results, and financial condition.

- *Stock sales*. Sales of substantial amounts of Ninja common stock in the public market, or the perception that such sales could occur, could adversely affect the market price of its shares. Any sales of common stock by Ninja or its principal stockholders, or the perception that such sales might occur, could have a material adverse effect on the price of Ninja shares.

- *Stock price volatility*. The company's share price is likely to fluctuate in the future because of the volatility of the stock market in general and a variety of factors, many of which are beyond the control of the company, including:

    o   Quarterly variations in actual or anticipated results of operations;
    o   Changes in financial estimates by securities analysts;
    o   Actions or announcements by the company or its competitors;
    o   Regulatory actions;
    o   Litigation;
    o   Loss or gain of major customers;
    o   Additions or departures of key personnel; and
    o   Future sales of the company's common stock.

    These fluctuations may result in an immediate and significant decline in the trading price of Ninja's common stock, which could cause a decline in the value of an investor's investment.

The SEC does not require an equally detailed discussion of a company's risk management strategy, which means that investors are only seeing the downside of the risk profile of a business.

A publicly held firm could see its stock price increase in relation to the shares of its competitors if it reveals its risk management strategy to the investment community. Risks can cause a company's earnings per share to fluctuate more than would normally be the case, so using risk management to mitigate changes in earnings increases the certainty of the earnings information on which investors base their buy and sell decisions. When risk management results in more reliable financial results, investors may be more likely to buy a company's shares, or at least be less likely to sell the shares.

The deliberate adoption of risk in order to enter new lines of business can also be communicated to investors. If a business adopts a new strategy that clearly involves taking on new risks, investors might react poorly to this news unless they are informed that the company is aware of this risk, and has taken specific steps to mitigate the risk.

In short, a reasonable amount of risk management disclosure gives investors a more complete view of how a business is being managed, which can improve investors' opinions of the ability of an organization to conduct profitable operations.

Summary

The areas of risk that are the clear responsibility of the controller are transaction errors and mistakes in financial reporting. However, a potentially more insidious risk area is the production of a corporate budget that does not reflect reality. If the controller does not object sufficiently to the production of a clearly unrealistic budget, the result can be a ramp-up in expenditures to support sales that will never occur, or ongoing expenditures in the face of declining demand. This is an area in which responsibility can be diffused across many departments, but where the controller is usually considered to have undue influence, and so can keep serious mistakes in judgment from occurring.

Chapter 8
Information Technology and
Systems Risk Management

Introduction

In some organizations, information technology (IT) is so fundamental to their competitive stance that they cannot operate without it. For example, airlines must have a reservation system that is functional 24×7, a bank must allow its customers on-line access to their bank account information, and a railroad must have real-time access to information about where its trains are located. If these systems fail even for short periods of time or are hacked, then an entity could be placed at considerable risk of failure.

In this chapter, we explore the different types of IT risks to which a business may be subjected, and how to reduce their effects. In addition, we note the use of procedures and controls to mitigate risk, and the circumstances under which they are needed.

Data Security Risk

If critical company records are stolen, made accessible to the public, corrupted, or destroyed, there can be serious monetary and business repercussions. For example, if customer records are stolen, the company must notify its customers, investigate and correct the security breach that caused the theft, and possibly pay a government fine. Customers may also depart as a result of the theft. Given the magnitude of these problems, one should be aware of the steps that can be taken to protect data security, which are:

- *Internal access*. Employees should only be given access to the data they need to conduct their jobs. They should be denied access to all other types of data. When employees change positions or leave the company, this should trigger an examination and revision of their data access privileges, so that unnecessary privileges are revoked. Further, databases should be encrypted. There should also be systems in place that track who is accessing information, what they are accessing, and the specific data being accessed.
- *External access*. Firewalls and password access should be mandatory for all external access to company systems. It may even be necessary to physically break any connection between a company's key databases and the outside world.
- *Portable data*. Keep close control over any data that is copied onto portable media. Track when it is taken and when the portable media are returned. All portable data should be encrypted.

> **Tip:** Create a reporting system that shows the data access privileges of every employee, as well as their job titles. A brief perusal of this report may flag excessive data access privileges, based on employee roles.

In addition, when any company operations are outsourced, the supplier probably requires some access to company data in order to complete its assigned tasks. If so, the company must extend its own data security procedures to the supplier, and periodically verify that those procedures are being followed.

> **Tip:** One of the best ways to deal with data security is to minimize the amount of data. This means promptly deleting data that is no longer needed, which requires an active data archiving and destruction program.

Ransomware Risk

Hackers may access a company's computer systems and then encrypt its files, requiring the payment of a bribe before they will unencrypt the files. Or, they can use their access to wreak havoc within the organization. This is a particular concern for organizations that cannot conduct operations without a functional computer system. For example, several facilities of meatpacker JBS were hacked in 2021, resulting in the payment of a $11 million ransom before the company could recover its computer systems and return to normal operations. Also in 2021, the systems of Colonial Pipelines were breached, resulting in the payment of a $5 million ransom after several days of being unable to operate its 5,500 miles of pipelines.

Reducing the risk of incurring a ransomware attack calls for a detailed analysis of every possible point of weakness that could be attacked, along with the installation of real time monitoring systems to detect the presence of hackers operating within a company's systems. This analysis should focus on protecting an organization's most critical activities, which can be expanded into other areas if there is sufficient funding available to do so.

IT System Failure Risk

A business may have a key IT system that must be accessible to customers with a high degree of reliability, or else sales will suffer. For example, an on-line retailer must keep its website operational at all times. Similarly, an airline must have its reservation system operational, or else customers cannot book flights.

This is clearly a major risk, and so deserves a considerable amount of management attention, and probably a large investment in risk mitigation efforts. Possible actions to take include the following:

- *Create a testing environment.* Set up a separate testing environment in which to test all proposed changes to the system, so that bugs can be identified and corrected before they are released on the production version of the system.

Also conduct volume testing, to ensure that the system can accommodate high levels of demand.

- *Install backup power sources*. Install backup power systems, which will be automatically triggered if the main power source fails.
- *Retain key personnel*. Identify the key positions in the IT department that are most closely involved with critical systems, and invest in retention efforts directed at these employees, such as increased pay, benefits, and training packages. Also cross-train these personnel and hire additional staff, so that the loss of a few employees will not be detrimental to running the systems.
- *Document systems*. Fully document how key systems operate, so that backup personnel can use this material to operate a key system in the absence of those staff considered to have primary operational responsibility.

The risk mitigation efforts noted here can be expensive, so it can make sense to limit these efforts only to mission-critical IT systems, where there would be an offsetting major revenue loss if a system were to fail.

Loss of Expertise Risk

Certain systems may require specialized knowledge to set up and maintain. If a person with the requisite skill set leaves the business and there is no backup person, the entity is at risk of having a system failure from which it cannot recover. It will then be necessary to bring in outside talent on short notice and at a high price in order to make the system operational again. Here are several ways to mitigate the risk:

- *Use Web-based providers*. The company can elect to not be in the IT systems business by instead shifting to web-based solutions. Under these arrangements, a third party maintains the software offsite and is responsible for making systems upgrades. The main downside is that employees cannot access these systems if Web access fails.
- *Use COTS software*. If the company confines itself to commercial off-the-shelf (COTS) software, it will not require an in-house development staff for that software. Instead, all upgrades are made by the software provider. However, this approach does not allow for systems customization. Also, the company is at risk if the supplier fails.
- *Develop expertise*. There may be limited situations in which a business must maintain a certain level of technology expertise in-house. If so, consider establishing a training program for the staff which incorporates complete training documentation, as well as policies and procedures. In addition, consider a heightened pay scale for the targeted individuals, thereby giving them less reason to look elsewhere for jobs. Further, target having extensive cross-training in the targeted skills, so that only a wholesale staff departure would place the company at risk.

Incompatible Systems Risk

An acquirer may buy another business that uses different IT systems from those of the acquirer. This can be a concern if the reason for the acquisition is to gain synergies by combining operations. When there is systems incompatibility, it will be necessary to either construct customized interfaces between the systems or engage in a complete systems replacement at either the acquiree or the acquirer. Here are a few risk mitigation techniques:

- *Incorporate into due diligence.* If having compatible systems is a major reason for an acquisition, at least put this point in the due diligence checklist. It may be necessary to give this requirement a high priority in the investigation, such as sending in a team specifically to review systems compatibility, and as early in the due diligence process as possible. If this group issues a negative report, then the acquisition review can be terminated without wasting the time of other due diligence teams.
- *Develop conversion expertise.* A serial acquirer may find that it routinely needs to install new systems at acquirees. If so, it can consider developing a high level of in-house systems conversion expertise, so that this issue is less of a challenge. An alternative is to build a close relationship with a consulting firm that can reliably convert systems for the acquirer.

Changing Technology Risk

There may be situations in which a new technology is being rolled out, but for which the customer acceptance level is uncertain. Or, the shelf life of technology has recently been quite short. In either case, there may be a risk associated with investing too much in a technology when it may be necessary to acquire replacement technology within a relatively short period of time. In this case, a financial solution is to make an acquisition using a lease. Once the lease expires, the company can shift to the latest technology, perhaps using another lease.

Leasing is also a good option when an entity is facing budget constraints, and so cannot afford to make a large up-front investment in technology.

Catastrophic Damage Risk

A business may maintain all of its IT equipment, software, and staff at a single location. This may be an efficient way to run the department, especially when the IT group is located on the premises with the rest of the company. However, if the building is destroyed or damaged, perhaps by a tornado or flooding, the organization's entire IT capability has just been destroyed. There are several partial and more extensive ways to reduce this risk, which are:

- *Backup data off-site.* It can be quite useful to arrange for automatic backups of electronic data to a cloud data center. By doing so, the data can be downloaded back to the company once the period of danger has passed and there are computers available to accept the download. Taking this step might also provide an incentive for a business to digitize a larger proportion of its paper records, so that this information can also be stored in the cloud.

- *Install backup power supplies.* Provide all key computer equipment with uninterruptible power supplies. Doing so keeps the equipment operational until it can be shut down in an orderly manner.
- *Enforce a backup procedure.* Test the automated data backup system to ensure that data is indeed being backed up at the designated times.
- *Elevate equipment.* Position as much computer and other electrical equipment as possible above ground, to reduce the risk of water damage.
- *Locate IT separately.* It can make sense to construct a separate facility for the IT group that is located well away from any locations prone to natural disasters.
- *Maintain a hot site.* The company can rent a backup IT facility that is maintained by a third party, or maintain its own backup site. This approach is most effective if the IT staff practices transitioning over to the backup facility on a regular basis.
- *Outsource systems.* It may be possible to use cloud-based solutions that are maintained by third parties. A localized disaster does not impact these providers, so employees can continue to access the systems from alternate locations, as long as they have Internet access.

GRC Software

A larger organization might consider investing in governance, risk, and compliance (GRC) software. This software is designed to show if a company is properly managed, takes appropriate risks, meets its compliance obligations, and properly disseminates its policies and procedures to employees.

A GRC system integrates a variety of governance, risk, and compliance objectives into an integrated set of software modules that may, in turn, be linked to various company databases. These systems can include the following features:

- *Environment, health, and safety.* The software tracks air emissions, waste discharge, greenhouse gas emissions, chemicals inventory, permitting, and performance metrics.
- *Financial controls.* The system can monitor controls compliance.
- *Internal audit.* The software supports any audit methodology in creating a framework for managing audits.
- *Risk management.* The system identifies risks, aggregates them across departments, provides incident tracking, and documentation of corrective actions.
- *Risk modeling.* The software can be used to monitor and model operational risks.
- *Rules engine.* The software accepts a download of a company's general ledger, and uses investigative rules to pinpoint areas of the organization's financial results and financial position that could pose material hazards to the

business. This rules engine can be used to engage in continuous auditing, where the system is constantly rooting through the accounting records as soon as they are entered into the system, looking for anomalies.

- *Survey publishing*. If a compliance organization requires that employees answer a specific set of questions, a questionnaire module can issue questions to designated employees regarding policies and procedures, which the system then aggregates and issues in a standardized report format.

GRC software is expensive enough to be out of range for smaller businesses, which must rely upon an assemblage of smaller, possibly home-grown systems for their GRC needs. Even larger organizations will find that the multi-month implementation and training time required for a GRC system may result in a lengthy payback period.

Note: A GRC system will not necessarily prevent a governance, risk, or compliance issue from occurring. The system can flag a likely problem, but an employee can still choose to ignore the issue.

The Use of Procedures

A procedure documents a business transaction. As such, it lists the specific steps required to complete a transaction, and is very useful for enforcing a high degree of uniformity in how those steps are completed. A procedure frequently incorporates one or more controls, which are designed to mitigate the risk of various types of losses. In some cases, an entire procedure is intended to *be* a control.

The Need for Procedures

Procedures are needed to ensure that a company is capable of completing its objectives. For example, the primary purpose of a consumer products company is to place reliable and well-constructed products in the hands of its customers. In order to sell goods to those customers, it must be able to complete the following tasks consistently, time after time:

- Log in a customer order
- Pick the goods from stock
- Assemble them into a complete order that is ready for shipment by the promised date
- Reliably issue an accurate invoice to the customer

A procedure is needed to give structure to these activities. For example, one procedure could instruct the order entry staff regarding how to record order information from a customer into a sales order (which is used to process an order within a company), which errors may arise and how to deal with them, and where to send copies of the sales order.

It is certainly possible for very experienced employees to handle these tasks without a formal procedure, because they have been with the company long enough to have learned how to deal with most situations through experience. However, such an approach relies upon the verbal transfer of information to more junior employees, which is an unreliable approach that gradually leads to the use of many variations on a single procedure.

Imagine a situation where there are no formal procedures in a company that operates multiple retail stores. Each store develops its own methods for handling business transactions. Each one will have different control problems, different forms, different levels of efficiency, and different types of errors. Someone trying to review the operations of all the stores would be overwhelmed by the cacophony of different methods. Further, it is evident that the lack of uniformity increases any number of risks – of fraud, inventory loss, incorrect customer sales, and so forth.

The Number of Procedures to Develop

Even a smaller business may have a large number of processes. How many of them really need to be documented in a formal procedure? If a business documents all of them, it may find that it has spent an inordinate amount of time and money on some procedures that are rarely used, and which must now be updated from time to time. To keep from making an excessive expenditure on procedure development, consider the following factors when deciding whether to create a procedure:

- *Auditor concern.* If the auditors have indicated that there are control problems in a particular area, it will almost certainly be necessary to develop a procedure that incorporates any controls that they recommend. Otherwise, the issue will have an impact on the auditors' control assessment of the business, which may require them to employ additional audit procedures that increase the price of their audit. In short, an auditor finding essentially mandates the creation of a procedure.
- *Risk.* If there is no procedure, is there a risk that the company will suffer a monetary or reputational loss? If this loss is significant, a procedure is probably called for, even if the procedure will be rarely used. Conversely, a procedure may not be necessary if there is little underlying risk associated with it.
- *Transaction efficiency.* There may be multiple ways in which a business transaction can be completed, of which one is clearly more efficient. If so, create a procedure that directs employees to use the most efficient variation. If there is only one way to complete a transaction, there is less need for a procedure.
- *Transaction volume.* As a general rule, there should be a procedure for the 20% of all transactions that comprise 80% of the total transaction volume in which a business engages. These procedures cover most of the day-to-day activities of a business, and so can be of considerable assistance in defining the jobs of new employees, as well as for ensuring that the most fundamental activities are followed in a prescribed manner.

The last point, transaction volume, is a key determinant of the need for a procedure. There are many low-volume activities where it simply makes no sense to engage in any documentation activities at all. Instead, allow employees to follow their best judgment in deciding how to complete a lesser activity. However, there should *always* be procedures for high-risk activities.

Deviations from Procedures

It may sometimes be worthwhile to allow deviations from procedures. An extensive set of procedures can be considered a straitjacket that is imposed on employees in order to force them to do business in a certain way. An excessively strong level of enforcement leaves little room for employee creativity, explorations of alternative methods, or responses to unusual situations. For example, a retail establishment might consider empowering its customer service staff to respond to customer complaints in any way they believe will most satisfy customers, rather than following a rigid procedure. This type of deviation might even be encouraged, as long as it meets a company objective, such as achieving greater customer satisfaction.

However, deviations from stated procedures are not practical or safe in many situations. For example, the procedure for creating a wire transfer should be rigidly enforced, since there is a high risk of loss if someone circumvents the approvals that are normally built into this procedure. Similarly, a fast food chain with many stores needs to have a food preparation procedure that is absolutely identical across all of its restaurants, so that food preparation can be achieved in the most efficient manner possible.

In short, most organizations will find that there are a small number of procedures that can be considered advisory, rather than mandatory. In most cases, however, it is better to roll out changes in a carefully planned and tested manner, which does not allow for any ad hoc deviations. The manner in which a business is operated will dictate which procedures will fall into each of these categories.

The Use of Controls

Accounting controls are the means by which we gain a reasonable assurance that a business will operate as planned, that its financial results are fairly reported, and that it complies with laws and regulations. They are usually constructed to be an additional set of activities that overlay or are directly integrated into the basic operations of a business.

A person who has been trained in control systems will likely want to install every possible control, and will then feel satisfied that he or she has saved the company from an impending failure. Those on the receiving end of these controls have a different opinion of the situation, which is that controls slow down transactions, require more staff, and have the same general effect on a business as pouring sand into the gas tank of a car.

Because of these radically differing views of the utility of control systems, it is useful to adopt a set of controls that are based on the following points:

- *Risk – monetary.* If a control can prevent a large loss, such as one that could bankrupt a business, then it makes sense to install it, as long as the probability of the event is reasonably high. For example, having two people involved in every wire transfer transaction is a reasonable precaution, given the amount of funds that could be transferred out in a single wire transfer. Conversely, if a control can never save more than a few dollars (such as locking the office supply cabinet), it is entirely likely that the sheer annoyance caused by the control greatly outweighs any possible savings to be achieved from it.

- *Risk – financial statements*. A business must understand its performance, and it can only do so with reliable financial statements. Consequently, controls over recordkeeping should be among the most comprehensive in the company. However, this does not necessarily call for an oppressive amount of controls in those areas where the amounts involved are essentially immaterial to the financial statements.
- *Repetitiveness*. Only install comprehensive controls for those transactions that a business will engage in on a recurring basis. For example, if a company sells equipment to a foreign customer once a year, and wants to hedge the outstanding receivable, a once-a-year transaction does not require an elaborate control system (unless the receivable is for a large amount – see the preceding point about risk). Thus, it behooves a business to concentrate on a finely-tuned set of controls for the 20% of its processes that make up 80% of its business (the Pareto Principle). Of the remaining 80% of the company's processes, those items involving the most inherent risk should be the prime candidates for strong controls.
- *Offsetting controls*. It may be acceptable to have weak controls in one part of a business, as long as there are offsetting controls elsewhere. For example, it may not be necessary to have someone sign checks, as long as all purchases are initiated with an authorizing purchase order. This concept can be used to great effect if there is a good business reason to keep one business process running as smoothly as possible (i.e., without controls), with offsetting controls in a less noticeable part of the business.
- *Cost*. The cost of controls must be balanced against the expected reduction in risk. This is not a simple calculation to make, for it can be quite difficult to estimate the reduction of risk that will be achieved by implementing a control. One approach to quantifying risk is to multiply the risk percentage by the exposure to the business, which is known as the *expected loss*. See the following example.

Conversely, it is easy enough to measure the labor cost and other factors required to implement and maintain a control, so there is a tendency for businesses to focus on the up-front cost of a control and downplay the savings that may or may not arise from having the control. The result tends to be a control level that is lower than it should be.

EXAMPLE

High Noon Armaments operates a payroll system that pays employees on a semi-monthly basis. When there are a significant number of data errors in the payroll, High Noon's payroll manager requires that the payroll be run again, at a cost of $5,000.

The payroll manager is considering the installation of an automated data validation software package that is expected to reduce the payroll data error rate from 8% to 1%, at a software rental cost of $250 per payroll. The cost–benefit analysis is:

- *No data validation.* There is an 8% chance of incurring a $5,000 payroll reprocessing cost, which is an expected loss of $400 ($5,000 exposure × 8% risk) per payroll.
- *Data validation.* There is a 1% chance of incurring a $5,000 payroll reprocessing cost, which is an expected loss of $50 ($5,000 exposure × 1% risk) per payroll. There is also a charge of $250 per payroll for the software rental cost.

Thus, there is a reduction of $350 in the expected loss if the control is implemented, against which there is a control cost of $250. This results in a net gain of $100 per payroll by using the control. Changes in the estimated probabilities can have a significant impact on the outcome of this analysis.

The resulting system should be one where some failures will still occur, but either in such small amounts that they do not place the business at risk, or where the probability of occurrence is very low. It is difficult to maintain this balance between controls and operational effectiveness over time, seeing that a growing business is constantly in a state of flux, expanding some lines of business, curtailing others, and installing any number of new systems. It is the job of the controller to watch the interaction of these processes with existing control systems, and know when it is an acceptable risk to pare back some controls, while introducing new ones elsewhere.

It is quite common to see a control system that lags behind the current state of its processes, usually due to inattention by management. This means that some controls are so antiquated as to be essentially meaningless (while still annoying the staff), while new systems are devoid of controls, and will only see new ones when a system failure occurs.

In summary, there is a balance between the system of controls and the efficient operation of a business that is difficult to manage. A good management team will understand the needs of employees to keep operations efficient, and so should be willing to subsist in some areas on control systems that may appear rather skimpy, as long as the tradeoff is between a notable improvement in efficiency and the risk of only modest losses that would have been prevented by controls.

Summary

Information technology pervades the modern business, and is absolutely critical to the operation of many organizations. Its sudden absence can bring many organizations to their knees, so this is considered one of the most important areas of a business in which to conduct a risk examination. The outcome of this review could very well result in significant procedural changes and extra expenditures to protect the systems and information of a business.

Accounting procedures and controls are built into many business software packages, and should mesh with the manual systems that feed information into and take the results from these software packages. The IT group tends to consider procedures and controls to be the responsibility of the accounting department, and so may not pay enough attention to how they are constructed. A better way to manage the risks associated with IT systems is for both departments to jointly examine systems and develop the necessary procedures and controls.

Chapter 9
Other Risk Management Topics

Introduction

There are several risk management issues that fall outside of the functional areas described in the preceding chapters. Risks can arise during the initial formation of a business, when the decision is made to operate in another country, and when forming an alliance with a business partner. A more general conceptual risk is to the reputation of a business. All of these issues are addressed in the following sections, along with ways to reduce the associated risks.

Investor Risk

When a business is founded, there is a significant risk that the investors will not only lose their entire investments, but also be personally liable for the ongoing debts of the organization. This situation arises when the founders do not give sufficient attention to the legal structure of the entity. However, the legal structures that can protect investors may also give them less control over the business, and could present income tax challenges. In the following subsections, we outline the advantages and disadvantages of the various forms of legal entity that can be used for an organization.

Sole Proprietorship

A sole proprietorship is a business that is directly owned by a single individual. It is not incorporated, so that the sole owner is entitled to the entire net worth of the business, and is personally liable for its debts. The individual and the business are considered to be the same entity for tax purposes. The advantages of a sole proprietorship are:

- *Simple to organize*. The initial organization of the business is quite simple. At most, the owner might reserve a business name with the secretary of state. It is also quite easy to upgrade to other forms of organization.
- *Simple tax filings*. The owner does not have to file a separate income tax return for the business. Instead, the results of the business are listed on a separate schedule of the individual income tax return (Form 1040).
- *No double taxation*. There is no double taxation, as can be the case in a corporation, where earnings are taxed at the corporate level and then distributed to owners via dividends, where they are taxed again. Instead, earnings flow straight to the owner.
- *Complete control*. There is only one owner, who has absolute control over the direction of the business and how its resources are allocated.

The disadvantages of a sole proprietorship are as follows:

- *Unlimited liability*. The chief disadvantage is that the owner is entirely liable for any losses incurred by the business, with no limitation. For example, the owner may invest $1,000 in a real estate venture, which then incurs net obligations of $100,000. The owner is personally liable for the entire $100,000. An adequate amount of liability insurance and risk management practices can mitigate this concern.
- *Self-employment taxes*. The owner is liable for a 15.3% self-employment tax (social security and Medicare) on all earnings generated by the business that are not exempt from these taxes. There is a cap on the social security portion of this tax ($118,500 in 2015). There is no cap on the Medicare rate – instead, the rate *increases* by 0.9% at certain threshold levels.
- *No outside equity*. The only provider of equity to the business is the sole owner. Funding usually comes from personal savings and debt for which the owner is liable. For a large increase in capital, the owner would likely need to use a different organizational structure that would admit multiple owners.

In brief, the unlimited liability imposed by a sole proprietorship is usually considered to completely outweigh all other aspects of this form of ownership. Its ability to avoid double taxation can be matched by an S corporation (as described in a later sub-section), but the S corporation also keeps the owner from being personally liable for the obligations of the business.

Partnership

A partnership is a form of business organization in which owners have unlimited personal liability for the actions of the business, though this problem can be mitigated through the use of a limited liability partnership. The owners of a partnership have invested their own funds and time in the organization, and share proportionally in any profits earned by it. There may also be limited partners in the business, who contribute funds but do not take part in day-to-day operations. A limited partner is only liable for the amount of funds he or she invested in the entity; once those funds are paid out, the limited partner has no additional liability in relation to the activities of the partnership. If there are limited partners, there must also be a designated general partner that is an active manager of the business; this individual has essentially the same liabilities as a sole proprietor.

A partnership does not pay income taxes. Instead, the partners report their share of the partnership's profit on their personal income tax returns. Because partners must pay income taxes on their shares of partnership income, they typically require some distribution of cash from the partnership in order to pay their taxes. If a partner elects to instead leave some portion of his or her share of a distribution in the partnership, this is considered an incremental increase in the capital contribution of that person to the business.

In those instances where a partnership recognizes a loss during its fiscal year, the share of the loss recognized by each partner in his or her personal tax return is limited to the amount of the loss that offsets each partner's basis in the partnership. If the amount of the loss is greater than this basis, the excess amount must be carried forward into a future period, where it can hopefully be offset against the future profits of the partnership. In essence, tax law does not allow a partner to recognize more on his or her tax return than the amount contributed into a partnership.

The key advantages of a partnership are as follows:

- *Source of capital.* With many partners, a business has a much richer source of capital than would be the case for a sole proprietorship.
- *Specialization.* If there is more than one general partner, it is possible for multiple people with diverse skill sets to run a business, which can enhance its overall performance.
- *No double taxation.* There is no double taxation, as can be the case in a corporation. Instead, earnings flow straight to the owners.

The disadvantages of a partnership are as follows:

- *Unlimited liability.* The general partners have unlimited personal liability for the obligations of the partnership, as was the case with a sole proprietorship. This is a joint and several liability, which means that creditors can pursue a single general partner for the obligations of the entire business.
- *Self-employment taxes.* A partner's share of the ordinary income reported on a Schedule K-1 is subject to the self-employment tax noted earlier for a sole proprietorship.

The risk associated with a partnership arrangement works well for limited partners, since their losses are limited to their own investments in the business.

Corporation

A corporation is a legal entity, organized under state laws, whose investors purchase shares of stock as evidence of their ownership in it. A corporation can potentially exist indefinitely. It also acts as a legal shield for its owners, so that they are generally not liable for the corporation's actions. A corporation pays all types of taxes, including income taxes, payroll taxes, sales and use taxes, and property taxes.

A private company has a small group of investors who are unable to sell their shares to the general public. A public company has registered its shares for sale with the Securities and Exchange Commission (SEC), and may also have listed its shares on an exchange, where they can be traded by the general public. The requirements of the SEC and the stock exchanges are rigorous, so comparatively few corporations are publicly-held.

The advantages of the corporation are as follows:

- *Limited liability.* The shareholders of a corporation are only liable up to the amount of their investments. The corporate entity shields them from any further liability.
- *Source of capital.* A publicly-held corporation in particular can raise substantial amounts by selling shares or issuing bonds.
- *Ownership transfers.* It is not especially difficult for a shareholder to sell shares in a corporation, though this is more difficult when the entity is privately-held.

The disadvantages of a corporation are as follows:

- *Double taxation.* Depending on the type of corporation, it may pay taxes on its income, after which shareholders pay taxes on any dividends received, so income can be taxed twice.
- *Excessive tax filings.* Depending on the type of corporation, the various types of income and other taxes that must be paid can add up to a substantial amount of paperwork.

There are two main types of corporation, which are the C corporation and S corporation.

C Corporation

The default form of corporation is the C corporation. It is taxed as a separate entity, for which the tax filing can be voluminous. Distributions to shareholders are made at the discretion of the board of directors of the company, in the form of dividends. A dividend is considered taxable income to the recipient (though it is not subject to self-employment taxes). This means that there *is* double taxation, where the corporation pays an income tax on its earnings, and shareholders also pay a tax on dividends received. Despite the double taxation disadvantage, the C corporation structure is heavily used, because it can be owned by an unlimited number of shareholders. This gives it an unrivaled ability to attract capital from investors.

S Corporation

A variation on the standard corporation model is the S corporation. An S corporation passes its income through to its owners, so that the entity itself does not pay income taxes. The owners report the income on their tax returns, thereby avoiding the double taxation that arises in a regular C corporation. Some additional points regarding the S corporation are:

- There can be no more than 75 shareholders, so this approach is most suitable for smaller entities.
- All of the shareholders must agree to adopt the S corporation structure.
- Every shareholder must be a United States resident or citizen.

- A C corporation or a partnership cannot be a shareholder, though estates and certain trusts and charities can be investors.
- There can only be a single class of stock, which prevents preferential payments and voting privileges.

Limited Liability Company

A limited liability company (LLC) combines the features of corporations and partnerships, which makes them an ideal entity for many businesses. Their advantages are:

- *Limited liability*. The liability of investors is limited to the amount of their investments in the LLC.
- *Income flow through*. An LLC can be structured so that the income earned by the business flows directly through to investors. This means that the investors pay income taxes, rather than the LLC.
- *Management*. An LLC can be run by professional managers, rather than a general partner.
- *Number of investors*. There is no limitation on the number of investors in an LLC, as opposed to the maximum cap on an S corporation.
- *Multiple classes of stock*. An LLC can issue multiple classes of stock, which can be useful when providing special privileges to certain investors.

The disadvantages of an LLC include:

- *Differing structures*. Each state has implemented different rules regarding how an LLC is structured and operated. This can cause confusion regarding the risks to which investors are subjected, how the entity can be managed, and its tax effects.
- *Filing fees*. There will be annual government fees charged to maintain an LLC entity, though the amount may not be excessive (depending on the state).

Summary

The corporate structure provides real risk mitigation benefits for investors, since it shields their personal assets from losses. Each variation on the concept has its own foibles, including differences in taxation, varying levels of control, and differing types of stock that can be sold. Consequently, we have noted the key attractions and problems with each, so that the reader can select the type of organization that most closely fits his or her circumstances.

Political Risk

A business may have operations in a country where there is significant political risk. For example, there may be a risk of unfavorable regulations impacting profits, or of the expropriation of assets. And more frequently, local protests over any number of issues could impact the flow of goods from a key supplier that is impacted by those protests. For example, violent protests in Chile in 2020 over the needs of the poor resulted in many businesses being torched, while protests against a military takeover in Myanmar had the same result. In both cases, exports from those countries were interrupted, even though the buying parties were not involved in any way with the associated protest movements. Yet another concern is the rise of systemic bribery in some countries. For example, the level of corruption in South Africa is alleged to have increased dramatically during the administration of a former South African president, Jacob Zuma, making life much more difficult for any businesses conducting operations there.

> **Tip:** It can be useful to compile a measure of net earnings at risk from operations in different countries. Also, itemize which company assets are most valuable, and which ones are also the most vulnerable to political issues; where these two lists converge is where the most potent political risk exists. Doing so can focus management's attention on where to mitigate political risk.

While political risk insurance is available, there are other alternatives. One option is to diversify the company's assets into other countries. For example, if it appears likely that capacity levels must be increased, should the company build the new production facility in another country and import the goods, rather than increasing the size of existing facilities that might be expropriated? This is a judgment that balances the incremental increase in costs from diversifying the asset base with the reduced risk of asset loss.

Another option with political risk is to integrate the company so closely with local inhabitants that the business is seen to be local, rather than foreign owned. This means giving high-paying jobs to residents, becoming involved in local charity events, and engaging in joint ventures with nearby businesses. By doing so, the local population has a good reason to intercede on behalf of the company. For example, a cruise ship company could purchase foodstuffs from the islands at which it docks, employ locals to staff its shore-based operations, and make ongoing donations to assist with local emergencies – all to build up a reserve of goodwill among the locals.

The "local" tactic should extend to forcing the facility's managers to live in-country. This allows for better information gathering regarding local political conditions. In addition, the managers can build up their networks of local business and government leaders, which yields even better information about what may transpire that could impact the company.

Alliance Risk

An organization may enter into a small number of alliances with its business partners. These alliances are intended to develop products and processes faster, create new distribution channels, or engage in research and development activities. Despite the initial intentions of both parties, many alliances fail within a short period of time. The negative effects of these failures include lost profits, lost intellectual capital, a reduced competitive position, and perhaps lawsuits between the parties. It is not easy to mitigate the risks of alliances, but the following approaches may work:

- *Use an escalated relationship.* If the timeline for developing a relationship is fairly lengthy, consider entering into a relatively minor relationship first, to see how well the companies work together. If the outcome is acceptable, gradually deepen the relationship with more cooperative ventures, to see how well the organizations continue to mesh. If problems begin to arise, an option is to back away from any more comprehensive alliance.
- *Conduct due diligence.* Use a modified form of the acquisition due diligence checklist to evaluate a potential partner, with a particular emphasis on compatibility. This is especially important when the partnership is expected to extend over a long period of time or if the amount of funds to be invested is substantial.
- *Place boundaries around information transfers.* The legal staff can ensure that non-disclosure agreements are signed, and that only the intellectual property needed for an alliance is actually shared with the partner.

Reputation Risk

Reputation risk is the possibility that the earnings and capital of a business will be impacted by an adverse perception of the organization by its customers, the investment community, or regulators. For example, the business press may uncover a long-running scam by a company's sales staff to inflate billings. The result can be lost sales, an inability to obtain additional debt from wary lenders, or perhaps a call by politicians to begin regulating operations. When investors hear about these issues, they are more likely to sell their holdings of a company's shares, so that its stock price declines.

A blow to an organization's reputation can come from many directions, and may be so unexpected that in hindsight it would have been nearly impossible to predict. Nonetheless, there are several ways to spot possible issues that could have reputational impacts, such as:

- *Examine business partners.* Other companies with which the entity does business may be engaged in activities that are considered questionable, such as employing child labor or strip-mining in wetland areas. If so, management should proactively consider dropping these relationships in order to avoid being associated with the underlying issues.
- *Review the industry.* Are other firms in the same industry currently being attacked due to specific issues for which the company might also be found culpable? For example, there might be a history within the industry of groundwater contamination. This is a particular concern when a group of activists appears to be targeting the industry; if one competitor has already been exposed, then the company will likely be targeted as well. This examination could result in immediate efforts to rectify the underlying problem before it becomes public knowledge.

A particular focus of attention with the customer base is the level of customer service that a business provides. If customer service levels are not settled on the first call or involve long waits, the reputation of the organization may suffer. Several alternatives are:

- *Overstaff.* Instead of staffing the customer service function for the average customer demand level, base staffing instead on a much higher percentage of the peak load. Doing so ensures that customers receive a response more quickly. Also, track the customer wait time obsessively and add more staff as soon as the wait time approaches or passes a designated threshold. The same concept can be applied to field service, so that customers do not have to wait long for a repair person to arrive. The costs associated with overstaffing are not minor, but can result in an excellent reputation that may translate into an unusually loyal customer base.
- *Use in-country staffing.* Using foreign customer service operations can be off-putting for customers, especially if the customer service staff speaks with a strong accent. By only using in-country staff, any customer interaction issues related to communications problems are eliminated.
- *Train employees.* The customer service staff should be sufficiently trained to be able to settle all but a small proportion of customer concerns with a single contact. This training may need to be continuous, especially in an environment where new products and services are constantly being released, each with its own issues.

Summary

For most organizations, there is not a great deal of political risk, since they do not operate in questionable political environments. Similarly, organizations tend to engage in few alliances. However, reputation risk is a constant concern for most entities; the reputation of an organization can be severely damaged through a single incident, and can be difficult to repair. Consequently, the management team should encourage a strong communications flow within the business and with customers in order to spot danger signs as soon as possible. A fast reaction to a difficult situation can defuse it before the contagion spreads.

Chapter 10
Contingency Planning

Introduction

In the preceding chapters, we have described how to identify, deal with, and measure risk – but what about the tactical ability to deal with an actual physical emergency? Perhaps an organization is subject to threats from flooding, fire, hurricanes, or tornadoes – how do we prepare for and react to these events? The following discussion provides guidance.

Contingency Planning

Contingency planning is a set of activities taken to contain damage and minimize injuries to employees. In the following sub-sections, we note many steps that can be taken to improve the ability of an organization to survive a major physical event. We begin with employee-related issues and then move to event detection and damage mitigation topics.

Disaster Communications

A standard approach to informing employees about disruptions to the business is the phone tree, which involves having employees call other employees to inform them of a situation. The callers may be department managers, or simply someone who is assigned the task. Consider giving employees a complete directory of all employee phone numbers, so that anyone can be involved in a phone tree.

A key concern with the use of phone trees is that many people only use cell phones, so the loss of cell towers in the area where employees are located will disrupt the phone tree system. In this case, several alternatives are:

- *Internal postings*. Post on the company's internal website the status of the business, as well as the contact information for those who can supply more detailed responses. This information should be kept on an internal website, so that the general public cannot gain access to critical operating information.
- *Texting*. The lowest-bandwidth form of communication over the phone system is to send text messages. These messages can sometimes get through when voice calls are rejected or dropped.
- *Bulletin board*. If the company's internet servers are not operational, consider shifting to messages on an electronic bulletin board that is hosted by a third party.
- *Rerouting*. Contact the phone company and have phone calls to the organization re-routed to an alternate location.

Disaster Drills

If there is a history of specific types of problems within the area, such as flooding or wildfires, then create a disaster drill that is tailored to the most likely event. The drill should be practiced at reasonable intervals (such as testing a flood evacuation plan at the start of the rainy season). These drills are not only useful so that employees know what to do and where to go, but also so that any flaws in the plans can be spotted and corrected.

Safety Procedures Training

Designate those individuals responsible for employee evacuations, as well as those maintenance and engineering personnel tasked with shutting down systems. Then conduct periodic training classes with them to ensure that they thoroughly understand evacuation and shutdown procedures. This training must be revised whenever building configurations are changed or employees move into new facilities.

Emergency Response Team

Designate a group of qualified employees to be the emergency response team, with responsibility to contain problems during their early stages before outside assistance arrives. This group should be well-trained in remediation techniques, and also thoroughly supplied with all necessary equipment, such as water vacuums, portable generators, and sand bags. They should also have access to a complete medical kit and be properly trained in its use.

Worker Flexibility

In the wake of a major disaster, employees may be able to return to the office physically, but they may be quite distracted by the effort required to reassemble their personal lives. If the entire area has been affected by a disaster, assume that a good portion of employee time will be spent contacting family members, arranging with contractors to make repairs, and dealing with insurance claims. Management should tone down its expectations for employee performance during this period, and also provide assistance by allowing for extra time off during the recovery period. It may even be more efficient to allow for *extra* time off, since this allows employees to settle their affairs more quickly and return to work.

Automatic Detection Systems

Fire and water detection systems are a normal part of the local building code, and also make sense from a contingency planning perspective. Even when it is not necessary to install detection equipment in order to comply with the building code, consider adding detectors wherever they can give early warning of a potential problem. In addition, conduct a periodic inspection of all detectors to verify that they are all functioning properly.

Preventive Maintenance

The use of preventive maintenance has been touted as a key tool for increasing the productive capacity of a business, but it also has a major side benefit – fewer dangerous equipment failures. When equipment is periodically inspected as part of an ongoing program of preventive maintenance, potentially dangerous incipient failures can be detected and corrected.

Boiler-Related Activities

Boiler failures tend to be catastrophic, so a number of preventive measures are needed. For example, verify that automatic shutoff valves are installed on all incoming lines, so that an explosion will not be rendered worse by additional water or fuel. These valves should be tested regularly. Also, develop a list of local boiler repair and welding firms, along with their contact information, so that they can be brought in to effect repairs. Finally – and most importantly – conduct regular inspections of the boiler, using the most conservative intervals recommended by the manufacturer.

Hazardous Materials

When a business uses hazardous materials as part of its ongoing operations, there should be an examination of how they are stored, to see if these items can be properly secured in the event of an emergency. For example:

- *Covers*. Ensure that all containers for hazardous materials are properly covered, so that a sudden imbalance (such as would be caused by an earthquake) would not cause a spill.
- *Dikes*. Build dikes around hazardous materials storage locations, so that spills can still be contained.
- *Containment supplies*. Maintain containment supplies near hazardous materials storage areas, such as absorbent materials, gloves, and empty containers.

Mechanical Drawings

In the event of a major emergency, it may be necessary to shut off water lines, gas lines, feed lines from hazardous materials tanks, and so forth. If so, prepare mechanical drawings of these systems and store them in several readily-accessible locations. Ideally, note the system shutoff points on these drawings, and how to reach them.

Equipment Positioning

In a flood-prone environment, position vulnerable equipment and inventory off the floor. In an earthquake-prone environment, position towers, utility poles, and signs away from buildings so that they cannot collapse onto these structures. Also, anchor or brace equipment so that it will not fall over or collapse.

Safe Room

A well-designed safe room can provide a significant improvement in safety to employees. A safe room should have dense walls, sufficient water, food, and first aid supplies for a short stay, enough space to accommodate all employees, and also enough ancillary space in which to retain the most crucial records.

Flood Mitigation Activities

In flood-prone areas, install water pumps in all basement areas. Also, consider building floodwalls around key buildings. Where possible, shift the most vulnerable equipment and inventory onto the higher floors of buildings. Further, adopt a procedure for regularly cleaning gutters and drains, so that rainwater is properly routed away from the building.

Hurricane Mitigation Activities

In addition to the flood mitigation activities just noted, create covers to place over all windows. This prevents window breakage, as well as the entry of rain into the facility.

Replacement Facilities

It may be necessary to open a replacement facility if an existing company location is destroyed. At a minimum, consider having an off-site location to which the company's information technology department can switch on short notice. If the information systems continue to be available, then employees may be able to work from home. This approach works best in a knowledge industry such as consulting or auditing services.

Summary

The points made in this chapter can be used as the basis for an action plan that improves the ability of a business to survive a major emergency. The exact contents of this plan will vary substantially, depending on the circumstances. For example, a business located in a seriously flood-prone area may need to develop several possible evacuation routes from the facility, while an entity located in a tornado-prone area may need to provide employees with a map that lists all local storm shelters.

Even if an organization has developed a truly excellent contingency plan, be sure to evaluate it at regular intervals, since the circumstances may mandate an alteration to the plan. For example, a recent buildout of the corporate headquarters may call for a different fire drill evacuation route, or the installation of new production equipment may have introduced additional gas lines into the facility, for which the shutoff valves should be noted in the plan.

Chapter 11
Insurance

Introduction

Insurance is a contractual arrangement in which an organization pays an insurance carrier in exchange for the assumption of risk by the carrier. The arrangement is used by a business when it wishes to offload risk that it does not want to or cannot retain internally. A carrier takes on the risk of many entities, because a large pool of risk exposures results in a highly predictable total payout, which can then be used to accurately set insurance prices.

Insurance is designed for events that are infrequent and high-loss. If events are too frequent, the cost of insurance coverage will be too expensive. If an event has small losses, there is no point in obtaining insurance coverage, since self-insurance is less expensive. Thus, insurance is intended for a very specific set of situations. All other types of risks must be dealt with in other ways.

In this chapter, we review the more common insurance policy terms and conditions, and then discuss the different types of insurance and their characteristics. We finish with several insurance-related administrative and analysis issues, including claims administration and cost management.

Insurance Policy Terms and Conditions

When buying insurance, an organization must be cognizant of the related contract terms and conditions, since they can greatly restrict the amount of coverage that a carrier is actually agreeing to. The net result of the following terms and conditions is that a carrier is limiting the extent of its maximum payout, avoiding certain high-loss events, and forcing buyers to participate to varying degrees in any losses incurred.

Deductibles

The typical insurance policy contains a deductible, which is an initial loss amount that must be absorbed by the insured party. There are several reasons why insurance companies impose a deductible, which are:

- *Frivolous claims avoidance.* The bulk of all losses incurred by an organization are quite small, and they would inundate insurers with these claims if the insurers were solely responsible for losses. The cost to investigate and pay these claims would be excessive. The deductible keeps these smaller claims from ever being filed.
- *Ownership of losses.* If insured entities can pass the full amount of losses on to their insurers, they have no reason to take action to avoid losses. By making

the insured parties responsible for smaller losses, there is a stronger incentive to avoid all types of losses.

Limit of Insurance

All insurance policies contain a limit of insurance, which is the maximum amount that the insurer will pay. This is needed by the insurer in order to avoid massive payouts due to catastrophic loss situations. Some of these limits of insurance are set quite low, so that the amounts paid out are inconsequential. If so, there may be little point in obtaining the insurance, since the amount of risk being passed off to the insurer is immaterial.

Co-Insurance

There may be a coinsurance provision in an insurance policy. This provision is designed to penalize the insured party if it under-insures the value of property. Coinsurance is stated as a percentage. The following example illustrates the concept.

EXAMPLE

Hodgson Industrial Design owns its headquarters building, which has a replacement cost of $3,000,000. The company's property insurance contains an 80% coinsurance clause, which means that the insured amount must be at least 80% of the replacement cost of the building, or $2,400,000. The actual amount insured is for $2,000,000. Since the insured value is less than 80% of its replacement value, a loss payout under the policy will be subjected to an under-reporting penalty.

The building subsequently suffers $500,000 of property damage. The amount paid to Hodgson by the insurer is calculated as follows:

$2,000,000 insured amount ÷ (80% coinsurance percentage × $3,000,000 replacement cost) × $500,000 loss

= $416,667

In essence, Hodgson pays an $83,333 penalty because it did not insure the full value of the property.

The most commonly-used coinsurance percentage is 80%. If the percentage is higher, the insurer is imposing a stricter standard on the insured entity to insure the full value of property.

Given the negative impact of the coinsurance provision, a business must routinely examine the values of its insured property to verify that adequate amounts of insurance are being carried. Otherwise, a loss could result in a significantly reduced payout by the insurer.

Exclusions

Insurance policies typically contain a lengthy list of exclusions. If losses are caused by one of these events, they are not covered by the insurance. The exact exclusions will vary by insurance policy, but may include the items stated in the following table.

Insurance Policy Exclusions

Earthquakes	Government seizure	War or sabotage
Flooding	Mold damage	Windstorm or hail
	Nuclear explosions or radiation	

Insurance Riders

An insurance rider is an adjustment to a basic insurance policy. A rider usually provides an additional benefit over what is described in the basic policy, in exchange for a fee payable to the insurer. A rider is not a standalone insurance product; it must be attached to a standard insurance policy. A rider is useful for tailoring an insurance policy to the precise needs of the insured entity. Examples of insurance riders are:

- *Life insurance.* An accelerated death benefit is added to the policy, so that a payout occurs when the policy holder is diagnosed with a terminal illness.
- *Directors and officers insurance.* A "tail" is added to the policy, so that the directors and officers receive coverage for several years following the normal termination of the policy.
- *Property insurance.* Additional coverage is provided for flooding, earthquakes, and fire damage, which may not be addressed by the basic policy.

Perils

Insurers may attempt to underwrite on a specific set of risks that they identify in the coverage; this is called *named perils* coverage. Since this type of coverage can exclude many types of risks, one should instead strive for *all-perils* coverage. Realistically, the cost of all-perils coverage may be so high that it is not attainable; if so, obtaining insurance devolves into an analysis of how to obtain the largest amount of named perils coverage for the lowest price.

Boiler and Machinery Insurance

Boiler and machinery insurance was initially designed to provide coverage for boiler explosions, but has since expanded to include coverage against equipment breakdowns (depending on the exact coverage purchased). A key benefit of this type of insurance is that the insurer provides safety inspections and loss prevention advice as part of its coverage. Because of these inspections, an insurance company can also suspend its coverage if a reviewer determines that covered equipment is in a dangerous condition.

There is an insurance loss under this policy when there is an equipment breakdown. The definition of a breakdown will depend on the specific policy, but typically encompasses a mechanical or electrical failure, or the failure of pressure equipment. A covered event should be one in which there is a sudden and accidental breakdown that causes damage to the equipment.

Quite a broad range of equipment may be covered by this policy, include heating and air conditioning systems, motors, telephone systems, office and computer equipment, compressors, and production machinery. Be sure to review the document carefully to determine which types of equipment are *not* covered.

This type of insurance is most commonly purchased by manufacturers, since they own a large amount of the targeted equipment.

Business Interruption Insurance

Business interruption insurance is designed to provide compensation to an organization if a designated disaster shuts down its operations for a period of time. This policy covers lost profits from business interruption, as well as the reimbursement of actual expenses incurred during the period when a business cannot conduct its normal operations. Though the probability of a major business interruption is usually low, this coverage may be critical when a claim does occur, and may keep a business from being forced into bankruptcy. It can be expensive insurance for manufacturers, which have a larger base of fixed costs to cover during periods when they are inoperable.

Policy Inclusions

The amount of profit to be reimbursed by the insurer is based on the amount of lost sales or customer orders, which are estimated based on historical sales information. The calculation of compensation can be quite subjective, involving the roll-forward of historical performance into the period of loss. The company's lost profits are then estimated based on the amount of lost sales and its historical profit percentage.

The amount of reimbursement under this policy is based on its profit history. If an organization has a continuing history of sustaining losses, the insurer will not reimburse it for lost profits, since there were no profits to lose. However, the insurer may still issue payments to reimburse the entity for certain fixed costs.

The policy will also reimburse the insured party for normal operating costs incurred during the shutdown period, including payroll. Depending on the policy, this can include extra expenses incurred that would not have been incurred if there had been no property damage or suspension of operations. Examples of these extra expenses are relocation costs and the incremental increase in costs required to subcontract work to third parties.

The reimbursement of certain costs incurred by the insured party may be subject to debate, depending on the circumstances. Examples are:

- *Advertising.* When the operations of a business have been completely halted, a case can be made that there should be no ongoing advertising expenditures until operations have been re-started. However, if the insured party uses advertising to sell off goods damaged during the event, this can be considered a loss mitigation cost, and so should be reimbursed by the insurer.

- *Depreciation.* This expense will not be covered to the extent that it relates to destroyed property, but should be covered for any assets that continue in operation.
- *Insurance premiums.* Most types of insurance that benefit the business are considered a fixed cost of operating a business. As such, they should be covered by the insurer. Conversely, any insurance intended to benefit a third party would not be covered.
- *Interest expense.* If a business is obligated to pay interest on outstanding debt, this is considered a fixed cost of doing business, and so will be covered.
- *Rent.* If a business rents a facility, and the rental agreement contains a clause not requiring rent payments when the facility is unusable, then this is an avoidable cost, and is not covered by the insurance. If such an abatement clause is not present, then rent is considered a fixed cost through the business interruption period, and so is a covered expense.
- *Utilities.* Charges for electricity, phones, sewage, and Internet access will be covered when there is a contract that involves ongoing fixed charges.
- *Variable operating costs.* If certain activities of the insured party have been stopped, then so too should the expenses associated with those activities. For example, the use of warehouse vehicles and delivery trucks may cease, in which case there should be a substantially reduced amount of expenditure for fuel. Similarly, if there are no sales during a stoppage period, there should be no commission expense.

Additional Coverages

Several coverages can be added to the basic business interruption insurance, which may be attractive options under certain circumstances. These coverages include:

- *Civil authority.* This coverage pays for business interruption losses caused by order of the local government. This usually occurs when damage to a facility forces the government to prohibit access to it for a period of time, typically for safety reasons.
- *Extended business income.* As the name implies, this coverage extends the period during which business interruption coverage applies, up until operations return to normal. This coverage can be useful when there is a large fixed asset base that cannot easily be returned to its normal operating condition (such as an oil refinery).

Management Actions

An organization can take several steps to improve its interactions with the insurer following the filing of a claim, including the following:

- *Mitigate insurance cost.* There are several actions that management can take to reduce the cost of business interruption insurance. For example, it can install sprinkler systems to suppress fires, adopt fire-resistant construction materials, and use safety procedures such as 24×7 patrols of the facility to detect in-process fires or flooding. Another option is to have multiple facilities among which capacity usage can be shifted, so that the shutdown of one facility will not have an undue impact on the entity as a whole. The same concept can be applied to the dispersed storage of inventory, so that the destruction of one warehouse will not completely eliminate all available stocks. All of these issues should be pointed out to the insurer when it formulates the insurance quote.

- *Maintain off-site records*. The impact of a disaster implies that an organization's records might be destroyed, which makes it quite difficult to calculate lost profits. To improve the situation, store financial records in the cloud or in a secure off-site location.

- *Return to full performance*. A requirement of this policy is that the insured entity must make its best efforts to reduce the amount of its losses from a disaster. This calls for active management of the situation to promptly protect damaged property from the elements, and to return to normal productive operations within a reasonable period of time. This may call for a detailed contingency plan to subcontract work elsewhere, sublease alternate working space, and so forth, run by a properly organized loss recovery team with members from all key areas of the business.

- *Documentation of mitigation costs*. When a business is actively engaged in mitigating its losses from a business interruption, the accounting staff must collect and organize all related billings. If internal company labor is used, the staff should keep track of the hours worked and the cost of this labor. The information is then forwarded to the insurer for reimbursement. If the documentation process is disorganized, it is quite likely that some expenditures will never be reimbursed, or that the insurer will question certain submitted items for which the associated documentation is poor or nonexistent.

Tip: Review the larger remediation expenses with the insurance adjuster before accepting supplier quotes, since the adjuster may disagree with the assertion that these expenses will be reimbursed. Doing so will prevent a company from incurring obligations and later finding that it does not have the cash to pay for them.

The best efforts clause just described also means that the insured party cannot simply abandon a property and effectively turn it over to the insurer.

Commercial Automobile Insurance

This policy covers damage to the vehicles used in a business, as well as injuries to third parties caused by those vehicles. This coverage may not be necessary, if a company does not own vehicles or has employees use their own vehicles on company business.

The core coverage is comprehensive coverage, which (despite the name) does not provide protection from the collision of an auto with another object; that requires the additional purchase of collision coverage. It is also possible to acquire special perils coverage for such events as fire, explosion, theft, hail, flooding, and vandalism.

A truckers policy is available that is designed for long-haul truckers. It provides liability, physical damage, and medical payments coverage. Pricing is based on vehicle size, the intensity of usage, and the radius of operation.

Commercial Crime Insurance

This policy covers a business against losses arising from a number of criminal activities. The insured party can select from several possible coverages, each of which provides a specific type of loss protection. These coverages are:

- *Employee theft.* The theft of property by employees.
- *Forgery or alteration.* Losses due to the forgery or alteration of checks or similar documents.
- *Inside the premises.* The theft of money and securities held on the premises of the insured party. Also, the taking of money or other valuables on the premises by force; includes shoplifting and safe burglary.
- *Outside the premises.* The taking of money or other valuables outside the premises, such as from an armored car.
- *Computer fraud.* The fraudulent transfer of property by use of a computer.
- *Funds transfer fraud.* The loss of funds and securities from the account of the insured party at a bank, due to fraudulent transfer instructions.
- *Money orders and counterfeit money.* The loss of funds from money orders that are not paid, and from counterfeit money that was accepted in a commercial transaction.

In determining the amount of a loss, securities are valued at their market value on the date of loss discovery, while property is valued at the cost to replace it.

Commercial General Liability Insurance

Commercial general liability insurance provides coverage for a number of possible events, such as claims arising from bodily injury, personal injury, and damage to property that is caused by the operations or products of a business. The two main types of coverage that can be purchased are:

- *Premises coverage.* Pays for losses arising from events occurring at a business location that result in third party claims.
- *Products coverage.* Pays for losses arising from injuries and property damage caused by company products that result in third party claims.

General liability insurance may contain coverage exclusions, so be sure to review the proposed policy with care.

Another consideration when buying this type of insurance is to determine whether it is a claims-made or occurrence policy. A *claims-made* policy only provides coverage for claims made during a specific date range. An *occurrence* policy provides coverage for events occurring within a specific date range. Thus, a claims-made policy focuses on the date of the claim, while an occurrence policy focuses on the date of the triggering event.

Some customers may require that their suppliers have commercial general liability insurance, especially when large contracts are involved, so this is usually considered a mandatory type of insurance.

Credit Insurance

A business may find that it can shift some of the risk associated with its accounts receivable to a firm that provides credit insurance. Under a credit insurance policy, the insurer protects the seller against customer nonpayment. The insurer should be willing to provide coverage against customer nonpayment if a proposed customer clears its internal review process. Credit insurance offers the following benefits:

- *Increased credit.* A company may be able to increase the credit levels offered to its customers, thereby potentially increasing revenue.
- *Faster international deals.* An international sale might normally be delayed while the parties arrange a letter of credit, but can be completed faster with credit insurance.
- *Custom product coverage.* The insurance can cover the shipment of custom-made products, in case customers cancel their orders prior to delivery.
- *Reduced credit staff.* Credit insurance essentially shifts risk away from a business, so it is especially beneficial in companies that have an understaffed credit department that cannot adequately keep track of customer credit levels.
- *Knowledge.* A credit insurance firm specializes in the risk characteristics of various industries, and so may have deep knowledge about the risk profiles of individual customers, as well as aggregations of customers by region. This information is a useful supplement to other sources of information about customers.
- *Tax deductibility.* Credit insurance premiums are immediately deductible for tax purposes, whereas the allowance for doubtful accounts is only deductible when specific bad debts are recognized.

Be sure to examine the terms of a credit insurance agreement for exclusions, to see what the insurer will not cover. In particular, coverage should include the receivables of customers that file for bankruptcy protection or simply go out of business.

Insurers will only provide coverage for legally sustainable debts, which are those receivables that are not disputed by the customer. If there is a dispute, the insurer will only provide coverage after the company has won a court judgment against the customer. The issue of a legally sustainable debt can be a serious one if a company has a track record of disputes with its customers over product quality, damaged goods, returns, and so forth.

> **Tip:** It may be possible to offload the cost of credit insurance to customers by adding it to customer invoices. This is most likely to be acceptable for international deals, where a customer would otherwise be forced to obtain a letter of credit to pay for a transaction.

Insurers are more willing to provide coverage of accounts receivable if the seller is willing to take on a small part of the bad debt risk itself. This typically means that a customer default will result in the insurer reimbursing the seller, minus the amount of a 5% to 20% deductible. There may also be an annual aggregate deductible that requires the company to absorb a certain fixed amount of losses in a year before the insurer begins to pay reimbursements. Requiring a deductible means that the company continues to have an interest in only selling to credit-worthy customers.

For some customers, or geographic regions subject to considerable political risk, a credit insurer may consider the risk to be so great that it will not provide coverage, or only at a high premium. If so, the credit manager must decide whether it is better for the company to assume the risk of these sales, or to pay the cost of the insurance to obtain coverage. Also, if the insurer discovers that the company's historical loss experience with its customers has been excessively high, it may require such a large premium that the company may conclude that insurance coverage is not a cost-effective form of risk reduction.

Insurers may only be willing to insure a certain amount of receivables per year with some customers. If the company chooses to sell additional amounts on credit to these designated customers, the company will sustain the entire incremental amount of credit risk. To avoid the additional risk, it is necessary to track the cumulative amount of credit sales to these customers on an ongoing basis.

Cyber Risk Insurance

This insurance covers damage to or theft of electronic information, which is arguably the most critical asset in a business. Consider the damage to a business if its customer database is stolen, client medical records are destroyed, or product design specifications are damaged. Besides recovery costs, a business may also have to deal with privacy-related class action lawsuits and the loss of customers. Further, many governments require companies to notify every person whose personal identity information was compromised.

Depending on the policy, coverage may include the following:

- Loss of business income
- Data restoration expenses
- Cyber extortion expenses

- Litigation and regulatory defense expenses
- Public relations and consumer notification expenses

Management Actions

To obtain coverage, insurance companies will want to review the network security standards and related security procedures of a business. It may be necessary to upgrade the level of security in order to obtain insurance coverage.

Directors and Officers Liability Insurance

Directors and officers (D&O) liability insurance covers claims made by third parties against directors and officers, alleging that the directors and officers have caused damages by violating their duty. Examples of such claims are as follows:

- A competitor claims that the company has improperly hired away several key employees
- A shareholder claims that the company has failed to properly disclose financial information related to irregular accounting practices
- A limited partner claims that the company has diverted assets to several related parties
- Company officials are held liable in a trademark infringement case
- The owner of a nearby business claims that the demolition of a structure on company property damaged his own property
- The government claims that a company is liable for the illegal dumping of hazardous materials

D&O coverage is essential, since the personal assets of directors and officers can be pursued by aggrieved shareholders, vendors, customers, employees, government agencies, and other parties. With this insurance, directors and officers are covered for acting within the scope and capacity of their positions. Coverage includes defense costs, as well as settlements and judgments. Typical exclusions from this policy include fraud, criminal acts, known liabilities, and punitive damages.

D&O insurance is underwritten on a *claims-made* basis. This means that the policy currently in effect absorbs the liability for claims made, rather than the year in which the alleged wrongdoing took place. This aspect of D&O coverage can be a major problem for directors and officers, who have a five-year statute of limitations on alleged wrongdoing, and yet may no longer be with the company during the latter part of that period, and so have no control over the quality of the D&O coverage in subsequent years. It is possible to purchase insurance for retired directors and officers that addresses this problem. Realistically, most claims are filed against directors and officers immediately after the triggering event, so this risk may not be considered an especially large one.

Management Actions

An excellent supplement to D&O insurance is for a company to indemnify directors and officers in its charter or bylaws, thereby limiting their personal liability from the assertion that they acted negligently. This approach helps to retain directors and officers when a business is in difficult financial circumstances for various reasons, and is therefore more likely to be sued.

Additional Coverages

Coverage against the employment practices liability (EPL) can be added to D&O insurance. EPL coverage protects against damages related to wrongful termination, sexual harassment, emotional distress, and similar issues. If EPL is added to D&O coverage, the aggregate limit of the D&O coverage will be shared with the EPL coverage, which effectively weakens the total amount of D&O coverage. A reasonable solution is to pay for an increase in the aggregate D&O coverage limit.

Fidelity Bonds

A fidelity bond protects an employer from losses caused by the theft of money, securities, or property by an employee. Despite the name, a fidelity bond is actually an insurance policy. This type of insurance is most commonly purchased by organizations that own or handle large amounts of liquid assets, such as brokerages and securities firms.

A fidelity bond may provide blanket coverage for all employees, or it may provide coverage only for specific employees. The insurer may require that certain hiring practices be used by an entity in order to qualify for a fidelity bond, with the intent of screening out undesirable job candidates.

Inland Marine Insurance

This policy covers damage to commercial goods while in transit on dry land, as well as when the goods are in storage. This coverage may not be necessary if a company uses third-party carriers that also have this insurance.

The policy coverage has gradually expanded from goods being transported on ships to a large number of coverages that may not appear to have any connection to the concept of "marine." The following are examples of what may be covered by an inland marine policy:

Inland Marine Policy Coverage

Accounts receivable	Fine arts	Mobile medical equipment
Camera equipment	Furriers	Motor truck cargo
Communications towers	Guns	Museums
Contractor's equipment	Jewelers	Musical instruments
Exhibitions	Leased property	Valuable papers

There may be several exclusions from an inland marine policy, such as pilferage from a shipment, securities, and currency. There may also be exclusions for goods transported by air, or outside of a specific geographic region.

It is possible to buy additional coverage that covers the loss of samples carried by salespersons, equipment used by contractors, livestock, and goods sold on an installment plan or rented.

Life Insurance

Life insurance pays the beneficiary if the insured person dies. This can be useful in a business under two circumstances. The first is when there will be a serious financial impact if an employee dies. For example, if a highly-experienced salesperson dies, the organization could see a major drop in its order volume. Life insurance can be used to keep a business afloat while it searches for a replacement hire. The second situation in which life insurance can be used is to protect against the death of a sole proprietor. In this case, the heirs may need to pay estate taxes or the liabilities of the business, or both, and need cash from a life insurance policy to do so. A partnership might consider having life insurance on a partner, so that the proceeds from the policy can be used to buy out this person's heirs. For example, there could be a cross-purchase plan under which each partner buys insurance on the other partners, so that each partner can pay for his or her share of the buyout of the interest of a deceased partner.

Key man (or key person) life insurance is designed for use by businesses, where the insured person is an employee of a business and the beneficiary is the business. The term of the policy does not extend past the key person's employment period with the business.

Political Risk Insurance

This policy reimburses a company for the loss of fixed assets, net investment values (investment plus retained earnings) and sales and supply contracts that are destroyed by civil wars, taken through expropriation, or damaged by contract repudiation or regulatory changes. Even if company management does not believe this coverage is necessary, investors or lenders may force the issue in order to protect their investments in the company, though only if it is doing business where there appears to be a reasonable degree of political risk. The policy is particularly useful for businesses contemplating overseas expansion, or which have production facilities in low-wage areas.

Professional Liability Insurance

This insurance provides coverage for specific types of liabilities that are not available under a commercial general liability policy. There are two main types of professional liability insurance, which are as follows:

- *Errors and omissions insurance.* Provides coverage for those working with clients, where errors can be detrimental to the interests of a client, such as accountants, architects, attorneys, and consultants. These policies can be structured so that all members of a practice are covered by the same policy.
- *Malpractice insurance.* Provides coverage for those working in the healthcare industry, such as doctors and dentists. Coverage is intended for liabilities to third parties arising from losses caused by the professional services of the insured party.

Property Insurance

This policy protects against the loss of physical assets. The cost ranges from minimal for a services business with few assets to a substantial sum for an asset-intensive manufacturing facility. If a business has used mortgages to acquire assets, the lienholders will require that property insurance be purchased in order to protect their interests in the assets. This is usually considered essential insurance, since it provides coverage of what may be the largest assets of a business.

Types of Property

The coverage given by property insurance applies to two types of property, which are real property and personal property. *Real property* is defined as any property that is directly attached to the land, plus land itself. Examples are buildings and storage units, as well as improvements to these structures. *Personal property* is defined as being movable, and so may include furniture and fixtures, vehicles, and collectibles. Inventory is considered personal property, and includes raw materials, work-in-process, and finished goods.

Policy Inclusions

Damage to property is covered by property insurance if the causes of loss include fire, lightning, explosions, windstorms, hail, vandalism, a sinkhole collapse, or discharge from an automatic sprinkler system.

The insurance pays for the rebuilding of damaged or destroyed real property. Further, it pays for the value or replacement cost of any lost or damaged personal property. If a policy is paying for the value of an asset, this means the replacement cost of the asset, less depreciation. Thus, an older asset will have a significantly lower replacement value than a new asset. The amount paid may be based on the production capacity of equipment. For example, if a fire destroys several identical machines, the insurer might decide to reimburse based on a single machine that has the same production capacity as the group of destroyed machines.

Finished goods can be insured at their cost or their selling price. In the latter case, this means that a profit component is included in the coverage, which is similar to business interruption insurance. If the insured entity also has business interruption insurance, the value of this profit component will be subtracted from any business interruption insurance payments, to avoid double payments.

Personal property owned by third parties is also included in the insurance coverage, if this property is in the custody of the insured party and is located on the premises.

Policy Exclusions

A number of items are specifically excluded from a property insurance policy. Depending on the policy, exclusions may encompass the following:

- *Animals.* This depends on who owns the animals and how they are being stored. For example, horses boarded by the insured entity may be covered if they are kept in a stable.
- *Cash and securities.* This includes bills and coins, bonds, and equity securities.
- *Land and land improvements.* This includes roadways, lawns, underground pipes, patios, and parking lots.
- *Vehicles.* This exclusion applies except when the vehicles are being manufactured, held for sale, or stored.
- *Covered elsewhere.* This includes property that is more specifically addressed under another insurance policy.

Additional Coverages

There are a number of additional coverages that can be added to property insurance. They only apply to specific circumstances, and so may only be needed for shorter periods of time. If so, be sure to remove them during the next coverage period, so that the company is not needlessly paying for inapplicable coverage. Several additional coverages are:

- *Buildings under construction.* A building that is under construction may not be covered by property insurance. This situation can be remedied by adding an endorsement to the standard property insurance policy. The endorsement should cover materials, equipment, and temporary structures adjacent to the work site. For example, a general conflagration could consume nearby building materials and the on-site trailer used by the construction staff.
- *Debris removal.* This coverage pays for the cost of removing debris from a damaged or destroyed facility, up to a maximum cap. This typically does not include the cost to remediate pollution caused by whatever caused the property damage. This can be useful coverage when property is extensive, such as a large warehouse facility.
- *Fire department charges.* This coverage reimburses the insured entity for the amount of any service charges imposed by the local fire department for

sending its equipment to a covered location. This coverage can be useful when local ordinances require such charges to property holders by the fire department.

- *Pollutant clean-up.* This coverage pays for the cost to remove pollutants from the premises if the pollution was caused by the event that damaged the property. This coverage can be useful when a business stores pollutants on its premises. There is a cap on this coverage.
- *Property preservation.* This coverage addresses any damage to property while it is being transported to a safe location or being stored there. This coverage can make sense if high-value items are being insured, such as artwork.

Management Actions

There can be arguments over the number and types of assets for which reimbursement is claimed. To bolster the organization's case, it is useful to take the following steps:

- *Record contents.* Create a record of the contents of the business' offices, including digital photos, which can be used to substantiate a claim. This record will soon be out of date, so schedule an annual update of the report.
- *Store records safely.* Maintain all documentation pertaining to the purchase cost of assets in a fire-proof safe, or in a secure off-site location. It may make sense to maintain a duplicate set of records in an alternate location.

Management should be made aware of situations in which insured equipment is old, and needs to be replaced with more modern equipment. In these cases, an insured loss will only result in a payment that covers the old equipment, leaving the business with a potentially large funding shortfall to pay for the latest equipment. It is useful to periodically summarize this potential shortfall and recommend that a cash reserve or line of credit be maintained that can be used to cover the difference.

Surplus Lines Insurance

A surplus lines policy is one that protects against a financial risk that a normal insurer is incapable of accepting, for any of the following reasons:

- A very high insurance limit is needed
- The risk is extremely specialized
- The risk has such unfavorable attributes that normal insurers will not accept it

Given the one-off nature of these risks, a surplus lines policy is more likely to be a unique one that is constructed for a specific policyholder. Since there is more administrative overhead associated with this type of coverage and there is little competition, insurance premiums are usually higher.

An insurer that takes on this type of risk is usually one that has not been licensed by the state in which the insured entity is located; as nonadmitted carriers, these insurers have fewer restrictions on certain types of coverage and pricing requirements. Also, the insurance agent handling the transaction must have a surplus lines license in order to offer this type of insurance.

A concern when making use of surplus lines insurance is that there is no state guaranty fund from which a claim payment can be obtained if the surplus lines insurer is unable to make a payment. This is because the insurer has not been licensed by the state, so the state's guaranty fund does not apply to it.

Workers' Compensation Insurance

This policy is required under state law, and compensates employees for injuries suffered in the workplace. The advantage to these mandated programs is that state law does not allow employees to sue their employers for negligence related to workplace injuries, unless there is gross negligence by the employer. If there is a dispute regarding the amount of a settlement, it is usually settled through a state-run review process.

Management Actions

The pricing of workers' compensation insurance is partially based on the claims history of a business, so it makes sense to have an ongoing workplace safety program in place. This program trains employees in workplace safety, identifies potentially risky activities and locations for correction, and investigates accidents to determine underlying causes.

Insurance Distribution

There are several methods by which insurance is sold. *Direct writers* are insurance companies that sell insurance through their own distribution networks. Salespeople are only allowed to sell the insurance offerings of their employer. Other insurance providers sell through a network of independent agents or brokers, who typically represent the insurance products of several insurance companies. An agent is a legal representative of an insurance company, while a broker represents the buyer, and assists the buyer in shopping for the best combination of coverage and price. If an organization decides to work with an agent or broker, it should make a selection based on multiple possible criteria, such as:

- *Areas of expertise.* An agent or broker may have particular experience in certain industries, and provide advice in these areas. Evidence of expertise includes the resumes of its technical support staff and the types of clients represented.
- *Carriers represented.* The company may have good experience with certain insurance carriers, and so will only work with an agent that represents those same carriers.
- *Services provided.* An agency or broker may offer an array of services, such as claims management, on-site inspections, policy analysis, and loss modeling.

Insurance Company Analysis

When purchasing insurance, be sure to review the credit rating of the insurance company, to see if it has adequate reserves to pay claims if the company experiences a loss. The easiest way to do so is to look up the *financial strength rating* (FSR) of the insurer, which is formulated and published by A.M. Best. The FSR rating represents an assessment of an insurer's ability to meet its payment obligations to policy holders. The rating is based on numerous factors, including an insurer's balance sheet and financial performance and an assessment of its operating plans and management. The A.M. Best ratings are noted in the following table.

A.M. Best Ratings

Secure Insurer Ratings		Vulnerable Insurer Ratings	
Rating	Description	Rating	Description
A++, A+	Superior	B, B-	Fair
A, A-	Excellent	C++, C+	Marginal
B++, B+	Good	C, C-	Weak
		D	Under
		E	Under regulatory supervision
		F	In liquidation
		S	Rating suspended

Insurance Pricing

A number of factors impact the price of insurance. It is useful to understand the vagaries of these pricing drivers, since excessively high prices can mean that insurance is not a viable risk mitigation tactic. Insurance pricing factors include the following:

- *Recent loss experience.* Pricing can be based in part on the loss experience of an insurance carrier. This means that a prior history of significant payouts will likely lead a carrier to continually raise its rates until its cash inflows from policy premiums are sufficient to offset its continuing payouts. Conversely, if a carrier has a declining loss experience, it will be more likely to reduce its prices. These factors have nothing to do with an organization's specific circumstances, but can still impact the prices it pays.
- *New entrants.* A new entrant into an insurance market may set aggressively low market prices in order to rapidly gain market share. A business can take advantage of this pricing by switching carriers, but be aware that the new entrant's prices will probably increase in the near future, once it develops a loss experience.
- *Pricing base.* The calculation of certain types of insurance is based on the volume level of the insured entity. For example, the cost of workers'

compensation insurance is based on payroll costs, while liability insurance is based in part on the sales of the insured entity.

Managing the Cost of Insurance

Depending on the risk profile of a business and the types of risks being transferred to insurers, the cost of insurance can be quite high. If so, there are a number of steps that can be taken to keep this cost as low as possible, as described in the following sub-sections.

Insurer Messaging

If the cost of a particular type of insurance continues to rise over a period of time, this means that the insurer believes there is a high probability of loss and resultant payouts to policy holders. If so, and rather than continuing to pay the insurance, consider whether the company should restructure its business to mitigate the risk. After all, the insurer is using its pricing to tell management that a business activity is excessively risky. For example, if flood insurance rises to absurd levels, take this as a warning that the company needs to move its operations to a safer location.

Covered Items Analysis

Review existing insurance contracts to see if the company is still paying for the coverage of assets that no longer exist, or for inconsequential risks. Of course, a result of this review could well be an increase in insurance costs, if it is found that some assets are not being covered, or major risks are not being addressed.

Double Coverage Analysis

Compare the coverage of all insurance policies to see if the company is paying for different insurance contracts that provide overlapping coverage of the same asset or risk. If so, eliminate the overlap when the contracts are up for renewal.

A concern with insurance riders is that they can provide duplicate coverage, so be sure to examine the terms of the basic policy to see if each rider is really needed.

Unlikely Payouts

Many policy riders cover events that are very unlikely to happen. Consequently, make a reasonable estimation of the actual need for a rider before paying additional cash for it.

Non-Comparability

The terms and fees associated with riders are customized to the specific needs of the insured entity, so it can be difficult to compare competing insurance offers. Insurers can use the non-comparability of policy terms to build additional profits into their offerings, so be certain that riders are really needed before adding them to a basic policy.

Deductibles Analysis

An insurance provider may offer different prices, depending on the amount of the deductible that an organization is willing to absorb. The correct deductible to select can be calculated in a two-step process, which is:

1. Determine the historical average loss experience of the business, and multiply this amount by the proposed deductible to arrive at the amount of the loss that the business is likely to absorb at the designated deductible level.
2. Compare the estimated loss to the premium savings associated with the deductible. If the loss is less than the premium savings, then the proposed deductible is a good deal for the organization.

EXAMPLE

The insurance provider for Horton Corporation is proposing that the deductible on the company's commercial vehicle insurance policy be raised from the current $250 level to $500. In exchange, the provider proposes to drop the per-vehicle annual insurance cost by $50. Horton currently insures 30 vehicles.

To see if this is a good deal, a company analyst notes that Horton has had an average of five vehicle-related claims per year for the past decade. In all cases, the amount of the claim exceeded $500, so the full amount of the deductible would always be applicable. The increase in deductible would cost the company an additional $1,250 per year (calculated as five claims × $250 additional deductible/each). The cost savings from a reduced insurance premium will be $1,500 (calculated as 30 vehicles × $50 premium savings/each). Since the savings exceed the projected loss by $250, Horton should accept the proposed deal.

Job Classification Analysis

The cost of workers' compensation is based on the job classification assigned to each employee. For example, the cost of workers' compensation insurance is much higher for a production employee than for an administrative person, because of differences in the inherent dangers of these positions. Consequently, it is useful to examine the job classifications of all employees just prior to the insurance renewal date, to ensure that the classifications fairly represent the actual work of each employee.

Delayed Payments

Some insurers allow premium payments to be made at intervals over the coverage period, rather than in advance of the coverage period. If so, and there is no inherent interest rate associated with these delayed payments, take advantage of the delayed payment offer. Doing so allows the business to invest the excess cash and earn a small amount of interest income. A larger organization that spends significant amounts on insurance premiums may be able to impose this payment schedule on its insurers.

Self-Funded Insurance

A very large business is likely to have many more insurance claims than a smaller organization. With a larger number of losses, such a large enterprise has enough information to statistically predict its losses. When these losses occur with high frequency and a low cost per claim, there is an opportunity to reduce costs by self-funding claims from an established reserve. The cost savings arises from the elimination of the selling costs and profits that an independent insurer must build into its prices. However, the organization must now pay for the administrative cost of settling claims, and may also need to pay for legal representation to defend it against spurious claims. An additional concern is that the business may be placed in the potentially uncomfortable position of denying claims from its own employees, depending on the type of insurance.

Examples of situations in which self-funding works well are automobile damage claims and workers' compensation claims. These situations present little risk of major losses, so a larger business can likely absorb these costs as part of its ongoing operating expenses, without imposing any material burden on its profits.

In situations where self-funded insurance is used, there may be a low risk of large claims. If so, a business can purchase stop loss insurance that provides coverage once an employee's annual claims experience exceeds a certain predetermined amount.

An added benefit of self-insurance is the detailed level of information available to the company concerning the types of claims being filed. With this information, it may be possible to create risk reduction programs that target the types of claims being filed.

Captive Insurance Company

A variation on the self-funding concept is to create and fund a captive insurance company, which typically complements an organization's commercial insurance programs. This approach is less expensive than buying insurance from an independent insurance entity, which must include a provision in its pricing for sales costs and an adequate profit. There are also tax advantages to using a captive insurance company. Given the costs to set up and manage a captive insurance company, as well as the cost to obtain an insurance license, this approach is usually only cost-effective for mid-sized or larger organizations. A variation is the rent-a-captive approach, where several medium-sized organizations share a captive and centrally manage funds in order to reduce the total administrative cost per business.

A captive insurer can issue property and casualty insurance coverage, as well as health and life coverage. Further, it can be used to insure against liabilities that would be uninsurable through third parties, or for which the price of available insurance is excessively high.

Insurance Claims Administration

The administration of insurance claims is of considerable importance, since the response time to these claims can be lengthy, and there is a high risk of claim rejection if the paperwork is not filled out properly. This issue can be mitigated by adhering to a specific claims administration process.

The core of this process flow is a checklist of activities that must be completed before any claim can be filed. The presence of a checklist keeps the company from missing a key step that could interfere with claim settlement. Other steps should also be included to record the associated transaction and to mitigate the risk of future losses of a similar type. The checklist should include the following items:

- *Itemizations*. List the estimated cost, replacement cost, and appraised cost of each item to be included in the claim, as well as the sources of this information.
- *Cost buildup*. Aggregate all of the related costs sustained by the company during the event, for which it may be possible to claim reimbursement.
- *Adjuster contact information*. Pull from the records the name of the claims adjuster to be contacted, and verify that this information is still correct.
- *Internal notifications*. Notify those people inside the company who may need to record the associated loss, and/or notify investors or senior management of the situation.
- *Problem analysis*. Review the cause of the claim and investigate whether steps can be taken to keep this type of loss from arising again.
- *Asset protection*. Ensure that no further damage to the damaged asset can occur. For example, move a water-damaged asset to a dry location. Otherwise, the insurer will only pay for the amount of damage initially sustained.

To ensure that these steps are followed, institute an occasional internal audit to review compliance with the checklist.

It is possible that a company focusing on other issues will have a third party administer its insurance claims. If so, be sure to have a monitoring process to verify that claims are submitted accurately and on time, and that a high proportion of the submissions are paid out.

Summary

The amount and type of insurance that a business purchases should be determined at the *end* of a comprehensive risk analysis. By waiting for the analysis to be completed, management can first determine which risks can be mitigated or avoided through internal activities. Any residual risks can either be accepted or transferred to an insurance carrier. This approach should be repeated at regular intervals, and especially when the underlying business changes, so that incremental alterations in insurance coverage can be made.

Chapter 12
Risk in Financial Analysis

Introduction

There are all sorts of financial analyses that a business conducts on a daily basis. Most focus on very specific decisions, such as whether to lease or buy an asset, whether to build a component in-house or buy it from a supplier, or perhaps whether to invest in a joint venture. The trouble is that risk is rarely included in these calculations, which can result in skewed decisions that turn out to have adverse long-term consequences. In the following sections, we note how risk can be incorporated into a number of common financial analyses.

Price Setting

The typical business has a standard price point at which it sells each of its goods and services. In addition, there may be situations in which a customer requests a special price in exchange for a volume discount. If so, the standard analysis approach is to determine the incremental cost of the items to be sold, and to accept a price that exceeds this incremental cost.

The trouble with the incremental cost view of pricing is that it does not consider risk at all. There may be a risk of a bad debt loss or of a sudden increase in commodity costs that will unexpectedly boost the price of a product. Or, a customer may have a history of returning a certain proportion of each order for replacement under the corporate warranty policy. Other possible risk costs include:

- Hedging costs
- Insurance premiums
- Product scrap costs due to defects

All of these factors should be considered in setting a price. If these issues are ignored, then a business is probably underpricing its products, and will suffer losses on certain of these transactions. In addition, if a company is known to offer unusually low prices, it may attract a number of similar orders, resulting in a significant proportion of its sales having low profits or even losses.

EXAMPLE

Horton Corporation receives an offer to buy 300 units of its left-handed widget for $5.50. Horton's cost accountant investigates the cost of this product and finds that the variable costs associated with it total $5.00 each. However, a deeper analysis reveals that Horton's risk costs related to this widget total $10,000 per year. In the past year, Horton produced and sold 10,000 left-handed widgets, which means that there is an average risk cost of $1.00 per unit sold.

When this risk cost is added to the variable costs of the widget, its minimum cost turns out to be $6.00. Consequently, the customer's offer should be rejected.

Dividend Analysis

The board of directors of a business may decide to issue dividends to shareholders, either to attract investors or because there is a perception that there are not sufficient internal uses for the cash. In either case, issuing dividends creates an expectation among investors that additional dividends will be forthcoming, probably in about the same amount and at regular intervals. Consequently, the initial issuance of a dividend may turn into an ongoing obligation to return cash to investors.

The trouble with the decision making of the board is that it does not consider risk when setting dividend policy. If the earnings and cash flows of a business are highly variable, the entity should maintain large cash reserves to support operations during loss periods, which leaves little cash (if any) for dividends. If the board were to create a dividend obligation in this situation, the cash reserve would be drained by dividend payments. If a loss event were to then occur, the treasurer would have to obtain loans or sell stock in order to raise enough cash to keep the organization solvent.

The only situation in which dividend payments only have a modest impact on risk management is when the variability of earnings is extremely low – probably because management engineered the bulk of the risk out of the business.

If a comprehensive discussion of risk were included in a board's dividend debates, it is possible that dividends would be set at a lower level, and that those boards contemplating the initial issuance of dividends would delay that decision.

Capital Budgeting

Capital budgeting is the process of examining proposed investments in a business to determine which ones should be accepted. The most common tool used for this analysis is net present value, in which the multi-year stream of cash inflows and outflows associated with an investment are discounted to their present values. If the resulting net amount of these cash flows is positive, an investment is considered to be worthwhile. See the author's *Capital Budgeting* course for a detailed analysis of this method.

When net present value calculations are made, the key element is the discount rate used to derive present value. At a minimum, the discount rate is set at the cost of capital of the business. If the resulting net present value is positive, it means that a project is generating a return that will at least pay for the associated cost of funds. However, where is risk considered in this calculation?

In theory, the discount rate is supposed to be increased in situations where there is considered to be a high level of risk. For example, several percentage points could be added to the discount rate of a risky project, which drives down its net present value and so makes it less likely that an investment will be made. When using this adjustment, there are several issues to consider:

- *Difficulty of developing a risk adjustment.* It is nearly impossible to create a discount rate adjustment that accurately reflects the amount of risk associated with a project. Instead, this tends to be a guesstimate that is tacked on to the cost of capital.
- *Unexpected risk is not considered.* When an adjustment is made to the discount rate, it is usually based on a discussion of the more obvious risks to which a project may be subjected. Unexpected risks are not considered at all, so the total risk expectation for a project is too low, which means that the assigned discount rate is too low, and the net present value will be too high.
- *Blanket nature of risk adjustments.* There is a tendency for a single risk adjustment to be made to the cost of capital, which is then applied to all projects that are considered "risky". This likely means that some projects with lower risk will incur a discount rate penalty that results in an excessively low net present value, while the reverse situation will occur for those projects with higher risk.

There is no easy solution to the points noted here, though it is certainly better to develop discount rates that are more closely tailored to the risk profiles of specific project proposals.

Research and Development Funding Analysis

The funding process for research and development (R&D) projects tends to result in the funding of less-risky projects. The reason is that there is usually not enough cash available to fund all proposed projects, so a ranking system is imposed to determine which projects will receive funding. The ranking is driven by a discounted cash flows analysis, for which a higher discount rate is imposed on the riskier projects. Since this analysis tends to reduce the cash flows associated with riskier projects, only safer R&D projects are funded. The typical result is that a business pours more cash into the extension of its existing product lines, which are considered safe investments, and little cash into real innovation.

One way to break through this safety-driven selection process is to deliberately allocate cash to several classifications of R&D projects, of which one is for high-risk endeavors. The amount allocated to each classification will vary, depending on management's willingness to lose money on high-risk projects. In general, this concept will increase the probability that a business will come up with a breakthrough product that can lead to an entirely new product line.

When cash is deliberately invested in high-risk R&D projects, there will inevitably be a number of project failures, either because the results will not be commercially viable or because the project is an outright failure. The real problem is when there are *few* failures, because it indicates that the company is not investing in sufficiently risky projects, with their attendant high returns.

To determine the amount of project failure being experienced, summarize the total expense related to projects that have been cancelled (known as *R&D waste*). While this metric can be deliberately altered by delaying the date on which a project is cancelled, it can still provide relevant input into the amount of project risk being incurred over multiple periods.

Even when the allocation of funding into different classifications increases the odds of funding a riskier R&D project, it is still necessary to allocate funds *within* each classification. A possible approach for deciding between projects is to use *expected commercial value* (ECV), which amalgamates the probabilities of success into a more standard net present value calculation. The formula is:

(((Project net present value × probability of commercial success) – commercialization cost) × (probability of technical success)) – product development cost

---

EXAMPLE

Entwhistle Electric is considering an investment in a tiny battery for cell phone applications. There is some risk that the battery cannot be developed in the necessary size. Facts pertaining to the project are:

Project net present value	$8,000,000
Probability of commercial success	90%
Commercialization cost	$1,500,000
Probability of technical success	75%
Product development cost	$3,500,000

Entwhistle's financial analyst derives the following ECV for the project from the preceding information:

(((\$8,000,000 Project NPV × 90% probability of commercial success) – \$1,500,000 commercialization cost) × (75% probability of technical success)) – \$3,500,000 product development cost

Expected commercial value = $775,000

An ECV analysis will inevitably result in some projects not being funded. However, not being funded does not necessarily equate to being permanently cancelled. These projects might become more tempting prospects for funding at a later date, depending on changes in such areas as:

- Competitor actions
- Legal liability
- Price points for adjacent products
- Raw materials availability
- Technical advances

These factors (many of which are risk-related) could change over time, so it may make sense to schedule an occasional review of projects that have failed the ECV test, to see if circumstances now make them worthy of an investment.

Financial Leverage

The essential concept behind financial leverage is to increase the return on equity of a business by funding new projects with debt, rather than equity. Doing so freezes the equity portion of the return on equity calculation, so that any incremental profits generated by the debt-funded activities will automatically increase the return to shareholders. This is called *positive leverage*. If profits decline as a result of debt financing, it is known as *negative leverage*.

In short, when used properly, debt financing allows a business to increase the numerator in the following return on equity measurement, while freezing the denominator:

Return on Equity Formula		Effect of Funding with Debt
Net income	=	Increases when leverage is positive
Equity	=	No impact on equity

The concept is best illustrated with an example, which follows.

EXAMPLE

The management team of Grissom Granaries wants to invest in five barges and a tugboat, which it will use to transport grain down the Mississippi River. The cost of these assets is $10,000,000. The company expects to generate an annual $2,000,000 profit by operating the barges and tugboat. The company can elect to fund the purchases either by selling shares or issuing bonds at an interest rate of 8%. The current amount of equity held by the company is $50,000,000, and it typically earns $5,000,000 per year for an average return on equity of 10%. The results of the alternative forms of financing appear in the following table:

	Equity Funding	Debt Funding
Current equity	$50,000,000	$50,000,000
Additional equity	10,000,000	
Total equity	$60,000,000	$50,000,000
Existing profit	$5,000,000	$5,000,000
Profit from invested funds	2,000,000	2,000,000
Less: debt cost		-800,000
Total profit	$7,000,000	$6,200,000
Return on equity	11.7%	12.4%

Based on the information in the table, Grissom's shareholders can earn a greater return on equity by directing the company to fund the fixed asset purchase with debt. By doing so, the denominator in the return on equity calculation (i.e., equity) is held constant, thereby boosting the return on equity with profits from the new venture.

The preceding example illustrates the benefits of financial leverage at the simplest possible level, without also factoring in the beneficial effects of income taxes on debt funding. When a company borrows money, the related interest expense is tax deductible in most taxing jurisdictions, so the net amount of profit generated is actually higher than was indicated in the example. In the following example, we adjust the calculation to reveal the effects of taxation.

EXAMPLE

Grissom Granaries is subject to a 35% incremental income tax rate. The return on equity table from the preceding example is adjusted below for the beneficial effects of this tax rate:

	Equity Funding	Debt Funding
Current equity	$50,000,000	$50,000,000
Additional equity	10,000,000	
Total equity	$60,000,000	$50,000,000
Existing profit	$5,000,000	$5,000,000
Profit from invested funds	2,000,000	2,000,000
Less: debt cost		**-520,000**
Total profit	$7,000,000	$6,480,000
Return on equity	11.7%	13.0%

Once the effects of taxes are included in the return on equity calculation, Grissom's management sees that the return on equity has now increased from 12.4% to 13.0%, which makes the use of debt an even more attractive option.

If a company is not currently earning a profit, then the tax-deductible status of interest expense is a moot point, and should not be included in the calculation of earnings to be achieved through the use of leverage. However, it may be possible to include the tax effect if the current lack of income is expected to be of short duration, since tax losses can be rolled forward and applied as net operating loss carryforwards against future earnings.

In short, we have established that financial leverage can be a substantially beneficial alternative. However, there is also a downside to the use of debt. If the borrower cannot generate a net positive return on the borrowed funds, then the result can be a major decline in overall profitability, as well as some risk that the company cannot pay back the borrowed funds. The issue is illustrated in the following example.

EXAMPLE

The financial analyst of Grissom Granaries hears about the prospective sale of $10,000,000 in bonds (from the earlier examples) to pay for barges and a tugboat, and is concerned that the profits from this operation will be too variable to support payment of the related interest expense. As proof, she notes a recent study that the depth of the Mississippi River has been too low in four of the past 10 years in the area where Grissom intends to use the barges to support the draft of the barges. This results in a binary situation – either the company can operate the barges fully or it cannot operate them at all. In the latter case, there will be no income from the invested funds, while the company must still pay the $520,000 after-tax cost of the debt. If this situation were to arise, the result would be as noted in the following table:

	Debt Funding
Total equity	$50,000,000
Existing profit	$5,000,000
Less: debt cost	**-520,000**
Total profit	$4,480,000
Return on equity	9.0%

The table indicates that a combination of debt financing and a low-water season on the Mississippi will result in a net decline in Grissom's net income, to a point below the 10% that the company was earning prior to its contemplated investment in the barges and tugboat.

The result of this preliminary analysis should be a detailed review of the odds of low-water conditions on the Mississippi during the period when the related debt is outstanding, whether management wants to sustain reduced earnings during these periods, and also whether lower-draft barges can be obtained that would make the fleet usable even in low-water seasons. If management is risk averse, it may choose to avoid these problems by either using additional equity to fund the asset purchases, or by not investing in the assets at all.

Stated another way, financial leverage increases the fixed cost base of a business by adding interest expense. This means that the breakeven point of a business rises, so that additional sales must be generated in order to provide sufficient additional contribution margin to pay for the added interest expense.

In short, financial leverage can provide a boost to the return on equity by providing funding for the generation of additional earnings, but at the risk of incurring a debt load that may prove to be unmanageable if incremental earnings cannot be created.

Tip: If the company's debt agreements with lenders include covenants that will trigger the recall of loans, model the earnings scenarios under which the covenants will be triggered, and discuss with management the probability of occurrence of these scenarios under a leveraged financing situation.

The downside of funding a business with a large amount of debt is that positive leverage can turn negative under the following circumstances:

- Lenders will only issue funds at a variable rate of interest, and the short-term after-tax interest rate increases to the point where it exceeds the incremental profitability of the business; or
- Lenders reduce the amount of debt they are willing to extend, requiring a business to replace the funds with more expensive financing; or
- The company's incremental earnings rate drops below the after-tax tax rate charged by lenders.

Some of these circumstances may be combined during an economic contraction, where banks routinely cut back on the amount of funds they are willing to loan, while company profits plunge. These combined effects routinely lead to the bankruptcy of those firms that employed leverage too much during the good times, without regard to what would happen under more adverse circumstances.

Examples of situations under which financial leverage can be best employed or where it should be avoided are noted in the following table.

Financial Leverage Usage Scenarios

Condition	Favorable for Leverage	Unfavorable for Leverage
Barriers to entry	When it is difficult for new competitors to enter a market, there is less downward pressure on prices, so it is easier to earn a profit on additional funds invested	When there are low barriers to entry in a market, there is a risk that a new competitor will enter at a low price point, driving down profits for all existing companies in that market, and turning their positive leverage into negative leverage
Competition	A near-monopoly situation is favorable for leverage, since a business can more easily maintain prices	It is unwise to maintain much leverage when there is a large amount of competition, since it is more likely that profits will be driven down over time, impacting the ability to pay back debt

Condition	Favorable for Leverage	Unfavorable for Leverage
Interest rates	If money can be borrowed at a fixed interest rate, the company has no risk of a rate increase over the term of the loan, and so can borrow more funds as long as the invested cash can yield a return greater than the fixed interest rate	If money can only be borrowed at a variable interest rate, then there is a risk of a rate increase eliminating all positive leverage
Lending environment	If there is a credit crunch where bankers are retracting credit, it may not be possible to obtain funds at any reasonable interest rate	When the lending environment allows for easy credit terms and low interest rates, this is an ideal time to engage in leverage, especially if the funds can be obtained at a fixed interest rate
Product life cycles	When product life cycles are long, it is easier to reliably forecast profits into the future, so there is a low risk of an unanticipated profit decline	When there are short product life cycles, a company may find that its newest products are not catching on in the market, so it can no longer support the debt payments associated with its financial leverage

The senior managers of a company may elect to engage in a large amount of financial leverage, even knowing that the preceding factors will put their companies at risk of negative leverage. The reason may be an excessive degree of optimism, where they assign a lower probability of occurrence to the preceding factors. In such cases, it is useful to keep management informed of changes in the various factors that can contribute to negative leverage. By doing so, it may be possible to take early action to reduce debt levels enough to mitigate the effects of negative leverage before the business is imperiled.

Summary

In all of the preceding analyses, a lack of attention to the effects of risk can result in adverse management decisions. A key situation in which the outcome has a significant probability of threatening the existence of an organization is financial leverage. Too often, the management team sees only the beneficial financial effects of debt, without fully considering the many circumstances under which the use of debt is not appropriate. In this case, there should be a detailed examination of the many scenarios that may adversely impact a business, and especially its ability to pay back debt. If reviewed in detail and discussed thoroughly, it is more likely that debt levels will be kept at a prudent level, irrespective of the temptation to use it to boost the return on equity percentage.

Chapter 13
Risk Measurements and Reports

Introduction

It is not easy to develop a pertinent set of risk measurements and reports, since they must be tailored to the needs of the organization, and the risk profile of a business is constantly changing. Also, the existing performance measurement system is designed to give feedback about the historical results and financial condition of a business, rather than the risks to which it is subjected, and so does not provide useful information. Instead, new information must be obtained and configured into a usable report format.

The key factors to consider when deciding which information to report to management are as follows:

- Does the information relate to a key business objective?
- Does the information relate to the company's compliance with government regulations?
- Does the information relate to an event for which corrective action is needed?
- Is the information important to stakeholders in the business, such as investors and lenders?

In the following sections, we describe the core reports that most management teams will need to see, along with a selection of additional measurements and reports that will vary, depending on the type of business and the functional areas that it considers to be critical.

Core Reports

No matter what type of operations a business may conduct, the management team should always be provided with a periodic losses report and incidents report. The losses report notes the amount of money lost in the period from different causes, while the incidents report summarizes the incidents that occurred in the period, irrespective of the amount of money lost (if any).

Losses Report

All types of losses can be reported to management. These losses should be a central focus of the management team, since they should either be recognized as the offshoot of a high-risk strategy or as losses for which mitigation tactics might be employed. However, reporting losses does not mean that the report recipients should be buried with detail. Instead, pare away all minor losses that do not meet a certain threshold. Also, consider aggregating losses into different categories for easier perusal, such as losses linked to customer credit, commodity prices, and exchange rates. Additional useful information could be to track losses against expectations, both for the reporting period and on a cumulative basis. These extra refinements are useful for highlighting unusual losses that require further investigation.

Incidents Report

The problem with the preceding losses report is that it only focuses attention on activities that actually lose a notable amount of money. Other events may not immediately lose money, but could do so in the future, and so should also be presented to management. Incidents that might appear in such a report are the theft of inventory or petty cash, the filing of a lawsuit against the company, a network failure during non-working hours, an equipment fire that was immediately extinguished, and an employee injury that was covered by workers' compensation insurance. These incidents could be indicative of larger problems, so it can be useful to attach an analysis that points out trends or perhaps correlations between different incidents.

External Risk Indicators Report

The preceding core reports focus on issues within a business. They should be paired with another report that measures external conditions that could represent future problems for the firm. The intent of this report is to give management sufficient time in which to take action with risk mitigation activities. Sample external conditions to report are:

- *Changes in key foreign exchange pairings* (such as the U.S. dollar to Euro rate). This is a direct indication of changes in the cost of doing business in foreign locations.
- *Consumer price index*. Indicates changes in the inflation rate, which can impact the cost of materials and the prices charged to customers.
- *Construction spending*. Can be used to predict future gross domestic product numbers, since it is a major component of the economy.
- *Gross domestic product*. Provides a general view of the health of the economy. A downward trend can signal the start of a recession.
- *Housing starts*. Trends in the number of new residential construction projects started are indicators of a strengthening or weakening economy.
- *Interest rates*. Increases in lending rates negatively impact business and consumer spending, while strong rate reductions have the reverse impact.
- *Producer price index*. Changes in the prices received by manufacturers indicate variations in the rate of inflation or deflation. This index is from the perspective of producers, while the consumer price index is from the perspective of consumers.
- *S&P 500 stock index*. Gives a general indication of the direction of the U.S. economy, for which it is considered a leading indicator.
- *Unemployment rate*. Tends to confirm the direction of the economy, as it is considered a lagging indicator.

These items should certainly be plotted on a trend line, so that management can see longer-term trends in the data.

Insurance Claims Report

Some risk will be offloaded to insurers, so it makes sense to summarize in a claims report the types of claims made and the settlement amounts. By doing so, one can see the size and frequency of insured losses. It can be useful to issue this report as a summary page, with details on attached pages regarding the nature of the various claims. Management can then spot an item on the cover page and drill down through the attachments to locate additional information. A sample insurance claims report summary page follows.

Sample Insurance Claims Report

Claim Date	Claim Description	Event Location	Claim Amount
1/05/XX	Boiler claim | Steam valve broke and flooded area	Thornton facility	$48,000
1/28/XX	Auto claim | Rolled over in high winds	On Interstate 25	42,000
2/09/XX	Directors liability claim | Shareholder awarded damages	Headquarters	100,000
2/10/XX	Property claim | Hail damage to warehouse roof	Little Rock facility	63,000
2/17/XX	Property claim | Fire damage to office furniture	Miami office	15,000
3/07/XX	Inland marine claim | Sales exhibition destroyed in transit	In transit to Dallas	30,000
3/15/XX	Business interruption | River flooding shut down subsidiary	Omaha retail store	120,000

If there are many claims, it can make sense to not include in the report any claims below a threshold level. Doing so keeps the reader focused on the largest loss events.

An option to consider for this report is to also include the deductible loss that the company absorbed, as well as any additional losses for which no insurance claim could be made. If these amounts are minor, it may not be worth the administrative effort to accumulate the additional information.

Cash Basis and Accrual Basis Reporting Variance

The accrual basis of accounting is the standard method used for producing financial statements. It holds that revenue is to be recognized when earned and expenses when incurred. While this approach will generally yield the fairest view of how well a business is performing, it can be manipulated by fraudulent activities. For example, sales may be falsely recorded, thereby driving up profits. A way to gain a general sense of the presence of fraud in a business is to also produce financial statements under the cash basis of accounting, where sales are recorded when cash is received and expenses when cash is paid. It is more difficult to record fraudulent transactions under the cash basis, since transactions are based on the movement of cash.

When both cash basis and accrual basis financial statements are available, compare them and note the percentage differences in the various line items. A certain amount of variation based on the timing of transactions can be accepted as natural. However, if there is a spike or gradual ramp-up in differences, and especially when these differences do not return to their long-term levels, this is a strong indicator that the accrual basis financial statements are being manipulated.

Third Party Credit Ratings

A business may subscribe to a third party credit rating service. A credit rating organization, such as Experian or Dun & Bradstreet, collects information from many customers about their credit experiences with other entities, and also collects public information about liens, bankruptcies, and so forth, and aggregates this information into a credit report. These credit reports can be purchased with varying amounts of information, such as a credit rating, payment performance trend, legal filings, corporate officers, and much more.

The credit rating assigned to a business is based on the credit scoring methodology developed by the credit rating organization, which uses certain types of information and applies weightings that may differ from what a company would use if it were to develop its own credit scores. Nonetheless, these third party credit scores can provide a valuable view of how outside scoring analysts calculate credit scores.

A different group of credit rating agencies assign credit ratings to either the issuers of certain kinds of debt, or directly to their debt instruments. The three agencies that collectively control most of the market are Moody's Investor Service, Standard & Poor's, and Fitch Ratings. The treasury staff can use the ratings issued by these agencies to evaluate the risk of debt instruments that could be purchased.

The rating classifications used by the agencies vary from each other to some extent. The following table presents a comparison of the credit rating classifications of the three largest agencies. Debt issuances rated as investment grade in the table are considered suitable for investment purposes. The ratings classified as speculative are generally avoided by those entities looking for safe investments.

Credit Rating Comparison

Risk Level	Moody's	Standard & Poor's	Fitch
Investment grade:			
(highest investment grade)	Aaa	AAA	AAA
	Aa1	AA+	AA+
	Aa2	AA	AA
	Aa3	AA-	AA-
	A1	A+	A+
	A2	A	A
	A3	A-	A-
	Baa1	BBB+	BBB+
	Baa2	BBB	BBB
(lowest investment grade)	Baa3	BBB-	BBB-
Speculative grade:			
(highest speculative grade)	Ba1	BB+	BB+
	Ba2	BB	BB
	Ba3	BB-	BB-
	B1	B+	B+
	B2	B	B
	B3	B-	B-
	Caa1	CCC+	CCC+

Note: There are additional lower speculative grades than those listed in this table.

From a risk management perspective, the treasury staff may want to invest funds only in investment grade securities, and avoid any securities rated below that level.

Aggregate Counterparty Exposure Report

A particularly telling measurement is to collect from all parts of the company the counterparty exposure that exists between the entity and its business partners. The result could reveal that the company as a whole, including all of its subsidiaries, is at a high level of aggregate risk with certain business partners. For example, there may be a customer that buys on credit from several subsidiaries, for a total outstanding receivable amount that could place the organization at risk if the customer were to fail.

Aggregate counterparty exposure can be quite difficult to determine, since it must be collected from the accounting systems of each subsidiary, and the customer names used by each subsidiary may not be the same. Consequently, a certain amount of manual intervention may be needed to arrive at a reliable aggregate counterparty exposure report.

Staff Turnover

When the percentage of employees leaving the firm is quite high, this introduces the risk that key operational knowledge will be lost. A high level of staff turnover may be accepted as normal in some parts of a business (such as the staff of a fast food restaurant), but there will always be selected parts of a business where a high level of staff turnover is considered a serious risk. Examples are the accounting, treasury, engineering, and research & development departments. Consequently, it can make sense to track staff turnover in these selected areas, and adopt turnover reduction techniques when the turnover trend is too high.

To calculate employee turnover, obtain the number of full-time equivalent employees who left the business during the measurement period, and divide it by the average number of employees on the company payroll during that period. The calculation is:

$$\frac{\text{Number of departed FTE employees}}{(\text{Beginning FTEs} + \text{Ending FTEs}) / 2}$$

An issue to consider is the time period over which employee turnover is measured. In a larger company with thousands of employees, a single month may be an adequate time period. However, in a smaller firm, it may be necessary to use the preceding 12 months on a rolling basis in order to collect sufficient information to derive a measurement.

An additional concern is that the measurement may be skewed by downsizings or firings, which are not necessarily indicative of a real loss of institutional knowledge. These types of turnover situations can be eliminated when calculating employee turnover.

Alliance-Related Staff Turnover

An organization may have entered into a small number of alliances with business partners, perhaps to develop new products or distribution channels. These alliances require a considerable amount of cooperation between the employees assigned to the work by each party. Building trust between these individuals can be a long-term affair, so if there is a high level of turnover among the employees assigned to an alliance, this can have a strongly negative impact on the ability of the relationship to survive. Consequently, if an organization depends on alliances to survive, management should closely monitor the turnover rate among the staff assigned to these alliances.

Compensation versus Benchmarks

An underlying concern that can cause employees to leave an organization is their compensation in comparison to the standard pay rate for the industry or job classification. This is of most concern in those areas where there are knowledge workers whose departures would have a significant negative impact on the organization. For example, if the sales effort requires highly-trained sales engineers, measuring their compensation against a benchmark would give management warning of a potential problem area.

This measurement is particularly useful when the economy is coming out of a recession, since this is the time period when jobs are more plentiful and employees are therefore more willing to look elsewhere for more pay.

Duration of System Downtime

When the success of a business is highly dependent on its ability to be on-line at all times, a reasonable risk measurement is to monitor the amount of time that the system is not operational. This may require that downtime be tracked even by second, when sales will be lost when there is even the briefest period of downtime.

If there are only certain parts of the day when the system must be operational, or if the issue is critical only for one or a few departments, then only track downtime for these key areas. For example, if the main risk is in having the treasury staff blocked from accessing buy and sell trades, then only track this information for them. Using the same example, traders may only need online access during those hours when the financial markets are open, so downtime measurement only matters during these periods.

Security Breaches Report

Unauthorized access to the data of an organization may be catastrophic, especially in regard to its reputation if customer-sensitive information is stolen. Consequently, any evidence of a security breach needs to be forwarded to management at once. This is less a matter of restructuring information into a formal report and more of taking action as soon as a breach is detected.

A report can still be used in order to see if there is a pattern of security breaches, since this indicates a lack of attention by management to remedy the issue.

Error Rates Report

When there are recurring transactional problems within a business, these issues can impact customers and suppliers, eventually causing problems that could endanger the business. Here are several examples:

- Inventory is not logged in properly, so supplier invoices are not paid on the grounds that goods were never received. This creates conflict with suppliers, who refuse to fill further orders.
- Invoices are continually incorrect, resulting in customers refusing to pay until they receive accurate invoices. Cash flows are seriously delayed.
- Bank reconciliations are incorrectly completed, so that the actual bank balance is much lower than the company believes to be the case. Checks are issued based on the incorrect balance, resulting in checks bouncing. Suppliers then refuse to do business with the company unless they are paid in advance.

- The year-end inventory valuation is performed incorrectly. When discovered at a later date, the company is forced to restate its financial results, which reduces investor confidence in its reporting. There is a general sell-off of its shares, triggering a steep stock price decline.

The examples highlight the fact that many transactional errors impact business partners and owners, who can respond with actions that are adverse to the existence of a business. If these errors occur with a high level of frequency, the risk of adverse action from outside entities increases. Consequently, it is useful to maintain a report that notes the frequency and nature of different types of transactional errors. This report is especially useful when tracked on a trend line, so that any spikes above the normal error rate will be immediately apparent.

Number of Regulator Warning Letters

When a firm is in a highly regulated industry, it is at risk of being shut down or fined by the applicable regulatory agency. In this situation, a good risk measurement is to track the number of regulator warning letters received. Depending on the agency, there may be several types of these warning letters, so a measurement of the volume received could break down the amount into the different classifications of letter, based on the severity of each type of letter. This information could be tracked on a trend line, to identify any spikes in the regulator's level of disapproval.

A variation on tracking warning letters is to track the amount of fines imposed by the regulatory authority. However, waiting for fines to be imposed only makes management aware of a problem fairly late in the regulatory oversite process. It may be better to use warning letters as the metric of choice, since it gives earlier warning of issues.

Customer Complaints Report

Certain types of customer complaints can be excellent leading indicators of product problems. Since issues with products can lead to expensive product recalls, it can make sense to create a report that identifies product issues that customers have discovered. This can be particularly telling for newly-released products, where there is a higher risk that undiscovered design flaws could cause products to fail. A variation on the concept is to report on warranty claims, with a particular focus on product failures.

This report should be compiled and issued on a frequent basis, perhaps every day. The reason for doing so is to ensure that management can take action to remedy problems as quickly as possible.

Credit Limit to Credit Usage Variance

It can be useful to match customer credit limits to the amount of credit they are actually using, with a particular emphasis on those customers operating near their credit limits. If only this information is reported, it may simply indicate that some customers have unusually low credit limits. However, if refined further by also noting which of these customers are late or partial payers, the report can accurately describe those customers least able to pay back their commitments. The report can then be considered a leading indicator of potential future defaults, and can be used by the credit department to gradually scale back credit limits to reduce the company's risk exposure. A sample report format follows.

Sample Credit Levels Report

Customer Name	Customer ID	Credit Limit	Max Credit in Past Month	Percent of Credit Limit
Albertson Clothiers	ALB02	$25,000	$26,000	104%
Bombay Nightgowns	BOM04	40,000	38,000	95%
Charleston Formal	CHA01	15,000	14,500	97%
Denver Nightclub Attire	DEN03	80,000	72,000	90%

Volume of Derivatives Trades

A business that is cognizant of its financial risks may use derivative instruments to mitigate these risks, as noted further in the Treasury Risk Management chapter. However, the use of derivatives creates a new risk, which is that the terms of derivatives will not be clearly understood, and/or that a buy transaction may be mistakenly reversed, or vice versa. These errors could result in a significant loss for the business. As a general indicator of the potential for such a loss, track the total volume of derivatives trades. If a large number of these transactions are occurring, it may be time to institute additional approval controls on the buy and sell process, to reduce the risk of errors creeping into these transactions.

Bottleneck Utilization

A bottleneck anywhere in a business keeps it from generating additional sales. A key focus of management is to ensure that this bottleneck is fully supported and utilized at all times, which makes the bottleneck utilization metric one of the more important performance measures that a business can track.

To calculate bottleneck utilization, divide the actual hours of usage of the operation by the total hours available. Depending on how closely management watches this metric, it can be useful to re-calculate it every day. The formula is:

$$\frac{\text{Actual hours of bottleneck usage}}{\text{Total hours in the measurement period}}$$

While important, the bottleneck utilization metric does not track the profitability of the work being run through the bottleneck operation. Thus, it could be utilized nearly 100% of the time, but with only low-profit items being produced, a company's profitability would still be low. Thus, this metric should be used in combination with an analysis of the profitability of products.

EXAMPLE

Mole Industries runs a small production line that creates motorized tunneling devices for cable laying operations. The bottleneck in the production line is the paint booth. The paint booth runs for three shifts, seven days a week, while the rest of the production line runs for a standard eight-hour day, five days a week. Management is concerned that the paint booth will limit the production line's ability to expand, and wants to know what bottleneck utilization it has. The calculation is:

$$\frac{152 \text{ Actual hours of operation}}{168 \text{ Hours in a week}}$$

$$= 90\% \text{ Bottleneck utilization}$$

The calculation shows that there are only 16 additional hours of bottleneck time available, and it is likely that the paint booth staff will have a difficult time making those few additional hours available, given ongoing maintenance requirements. Thus, the management team needs to discuss whether it should invest in an additional paint booth or outsource some painting to a supplier. It may make more sense to build a new paint booth if there is an expectation of a large and permanent increase in sales (which would pay for the investment in a new paint booth), whereas outsourcing may be the better option if sales are not expected to increase much beyond the current level.

Reporting Thresholds

When discussing the previous measurements and reports, we frequently noted that only the most unusual or critical items need to be brought to management's attention. By doing so, modest levels of variability in results are ignored, while management can focus on the more unusual events or trends.

How is the threshold developed that determines which items are reported and which are ignored? This depends upon the risk tolerance of a business. A highly risk-averse management team will pounce on nearly any loss event, while others willing to operate in a high-risk, high-reward environment will probably choose to ignore many smaller losses. For example, a business operates in a low-margin environment where it cannot afford to incur many bad debts. Its bad debt reporting may require a reporting threshold of just $100 for bad debts. Conversely, another organization is in the business of buying questionable credit card debts from credit card companies for a steep discount, and attempting to collect them. This entity assumes that most receivables *will* be bad debts, and so will ignore most of them in its bad debt reporting.

A reporting threshold is probably going to be derived based on some experimentation with reporting. Initial reports can include a large amount of detail, for which the recipients provide feedback regarding how much higher the reporting threshold should be set in order to arrive at a reasonable amount of information. This will probably require several iterations before report recipients feel that the report contents are optimal. If this approach is used, deliberately set the reporting levels to a greater level of detail once a year, to see if management actually wants to see more information. The intent is to determine whether the circumstances have changed enough to warrant additional reporting.

Another way to set a reporting threshold is by modeling what would happen if loss events occur at certain threshold levels. The threshold level should be set at the point where management decides that losses are becoming material. The concept of materiality levels should be discussed with management at least annually, to see if their dollar value for materiality has changed. If so, this alters the threshold level at which items are reported.

Cash Forecasting

Most of the preceding recommendations for risk measurements and reports are intended to either give warning of impending risk-related events, or to manage areas of a business that are associated with high levels of risk. Cash forecasting is a different reporting issue entirely, for it is a key input into the risk mitigation efforts of the treasury department. We include it in this chapter in order to point out that the cash forecast must be as accurate as possible, or else hedges may be booked for incorrect time periods, or in amounts that are too large or too small. The outcome could be financial results that are harmful to the organization. Consequently, there must be a process in place for tracking cash forecasting variances and the reasons for these variances. A cash forecast reconciliation should encompass the following activities:

- Investigate items that were expected to occur, but which did not
- Investigate items that were entirely unanticipated, or which were accelerated
- Investigate items that occurred in unanticipated amounts

The result can be a formal reconciliation document, but the main point is for the cash forecast preparers to gain experience with any permutations in the company's cash flows. The gradual accumulation of knowledge about such matters as the speed with which certain business partners pay the company or cash its checks is key to the improvement of cash forecasts.

Summary

A good feedback loop for evaluating the effectiveness of a risk reporting system is to compare significant actual losses sustained to the reports in the previous period(s) to see if the losses were predicted. If not, is it necessary to add a report that warns management of similar losses in the future? The concept can be turned around to see if certain reports are falsely indicating future losses that never occur, in which case it may be necessary to revise the items reported or the reporting thresholds for these reports. By doing so, the quality of reporting will increase over time.

We have noted a number of measurements and reports that could be sent to management. However, the volume of information presented to management can be overwhelming. To focus attention on only those issues that really require attention, the person generating this information should sort through it and compile a compressed report that focuses attention on actionable items. All other information should be excluded, or only made available as backup information.

Glossary

A

Accrual basis accounting. The concept of recognizing revenue when earned and expenses when incurred.

B

Bottleneck. A restriction on the output of a system.

C

Capital budgeting. The process of examining proposed investments to determine which ones should be accepted.

Cash basis accounting. The concept of recognizing revenue when cash is received and expenses when cash is paid.

Claims-made policy. An insurance policy that provides coverage for claims made during a specific date range.

Claw-back provision. The recovery of money that had previously been disbursed.

Co-insurance. A penalty imposed on an insured party if it under-insures the value of property.

Co-pay. A fixed amount paid by an insured for each doctor visit or drug purchase.

Contingency planning. A set of activities taken to contain damage and minimize injuries to employees.

D

Deductible. An initial loss amount that must be absorbed by the insured party.

Discount rate. The interest rate used in discounted cash flow analysis to derive the present value of cash flows.

Due diligence. An investigation of a potential investment.

E

Enterprise risk management. A consistent methodology for locating, measuring, and reporting on risks throughout an organization.

Exempt. A job classification in which employees are not entitled to overtime pay.

Expected loss. The estimated amount of a loss multiplied by the probability of occurrence.

F

Financial leverage. The degree to which an organization uses debt to fund its operations.

Full-time equivalent. The hours worked by one employee on a full-time basis.

Functional currency. The currency that an entity uses in the majority of its business transactions.

H

Hedging. A risk management strategy used to offset price fluctuations.

I

Internal audit. The examination of an organization's activities and processes by an internal group of auditors.

L

Lagging indicator. An indicator that occurs after the economy has begun to follow a trend.

Leading indicator. Something that can be used to predict future economic behavior.

Limit of insurance. The maximum amount that an insurer will pay.

N

Net present value. The discounted current value of a stream of cash flows.

Nonexempt. A job classification in which employees are entitled to overtime pay.

Notional amount. The face amount used to calculate payments on a financial instrument, such as an option or interest rate swap.

O

Occurrence policy. An insurance policy that provides coverage for events occurring within a specific date range.

P

Personal property. Property that is movable; it can be defined as all property other than real property.

R

Real property. Any property that is directly attached to the land, plus the land itself.

Rider. An adjustment to a basic insurance policy.

Risk. Uncertainty regarding a future outcome.

S

Safety stock. Extra inventory that acts as a buffer between forecasted and actual demand.

Spot price. The price at which a currency can currently be purchased.

Stock option. A contract in which a person has the right, but not the obligation, to buy shares at a certain exercise price.

Supply chain. The network of suppliers that provide goods and services to a buyer.

T

Translation exposure. The risk of a reported change in value of a company's assets and liabilities, if they are denominated in a foreign currency.

U

Use tax. A sales tax that is paid by the purchaser of goods or services.

W

Work cell. A cluster of equipment and personnel that performs a specific task.

Index

171

www.ingramcontent.com/pod-product-compliance
Lightning Source LLC
Chambersburg PA
CBHW080549220326
41599CB00032B/6421